UPLIFTING

Inspiring Stories of Loss, Change, and Growth
Inspirited by the work of Dr. Elisabeth Kübler-Ross

DR. KATIE EASTMAN

BALBOA.PRESS
A DIVISION OF HAY HOUSE

Balboa Press books may be ordered through booksellers or by contacting:

Balboa Press
A Division of Hay House
1663 Liberty Drive
Bloomington, IN 47403
www.balboapress.com
844-682-1282

Because of the dynamic nature of the Internet, any web addresses or links contained in this book may have changed since publication and may no longer be valid. The views expressed in this work are solely those of the author and do not necessarily reflect the views of the publisher, and the publisher hereby disclaims any responsibility for them.

The author of this book does not dispense medical advice or prescribe the use of any technique as a form of treatment for physical, emotional, or medical problems without the advice of a physician, either directly or indirectly. The intent of the author is only to offer information of a general nature to help you in your quest for emotional and spiritual well-being. In the event you use any of the information in this book for yourself, which is your constitutional right, the author and the publisher assume no responsibility for your actions.

Any people depicted in stock imagery provided by Getty Images are models, and such images are being used for illustrative purposes only. Certain stock imagery © Getty Images.

Edited by Chris Murray
Photo credit for cover photo: Sarah Quinn

Print information available on the last page.

ISBN: 979-8-7652-4882-9 (sc)
ISBN: 979-8-7652-4883-6 (hc)
ISBN: 979-8-7652-4881-2 (e)

Library of Congress Control Number: 2024900557

Balboa Press rev. date: 02/27/2024

DEDICATION

To a lifetime of teachers, young and old, human and from nature, who have lifted me with your wisdom!

CONTENTS

FOREWORD
by Ken Ross, Son of Elisabeth Kübler-Ross

In the vast expanse of human experience, there is one constant that binds us all: change. Change and loss are intrinsic parts of our lives, weaving through the very fabric of our existence, both personal and professional. It shapes our destiny, molds our character, and determines the course of our journey. Yet, despite its inevitability, embracing change remains one of the most daunting challenges we face. It is with admiration and gratitude that I introduce you to a book that has, in my opinion, greatly helped to demystify the complex terrain of change: Dr. Katie Eastman's *UPLIFTING: Inspiring Stories of Loss, Change, and Growth.*

In a world that often appears tumultuous and unpredictable, *Uplifting* offers a steady hand, a friendly voice, and a wellspring of insight. Her career as a doctoral-level mental health professional with training in spirituality and psychology, and her personal journey through her own experiences of loss and transformation, uniquely position her to provide a perspective that is both professionally informed and deeply relatable. She understands that the change curve is not just a theoretical concept but a profound and often painful reality we must all face.

Change and loss affect every facet of our lives. They manifest in our personal relationships, our careers, our sense of self, and our overall well-being. Dr. Eastman's approach is holistic, as she recognizes that the boundaries between personal and professional are often blurred. She doesn't simply focus on the psychological aspects of change but takes a comprehensive view, addressing the emotional, spiritual, and intellectual dimensions. Her compassionate and comprehensive perspective provides invaluable guidance for individuals no matter where they find themselves on the ever-evolving path of life.

In her meticulously crafted book, Dr. Eastman navigates us through the intricate and often turbulent waters of change, drawing initially on the framework of the Kübler-Ross Change Curve. In her masterful exploration, she unveils the profound relationship connection between loss and change, illuminating their reciprocal relationship in a way that is both enlightening and comforting.

This book serves as a roadmap for individuals seeking to navigate the complex terrain of loss and change. Dr. Eastman's insights are like a compass, helping us chart a course through the stormy seas of change, reminding us that while loss is a part of the journey, transformation and growth are the ultimate destinations. It is a testament to Dr. Eastman's dedication to making profound knowledge available to all, and I am deeply thankful for her efforts in this regard.

In conclusion, *Uplifting* is not just a book; it is a beacon of light in the sometimes dark and uncertain world of loss and change. She guides us with grace and wisdom, reminding us that these intertwined elements are not adversaries but companions on our journey. I have no doubt that her words will inspire, guide, and empower you as they have for so many others in her long career. So, let us embark on this enlightening journey together, knowing that we are in the capable hands of a true expert in the field.

Thank you, Katie, for sharing your wisdom, insights, and guidance through this complex challenge that so many of us face.

Your work is a tribute to the transformative power of knowledge and empathy.

Ken Ross
Elisabeth Kübler-Ross Foundation President
October 2023

PREFACE
A letter to my greatest teachers, who inspire me every day

Dear Cali, my loving daughter, and John, my beloved husband:
My Sweet Ones,

This book is for you and everyone facing the inevitable loss and changes that occur when something or someone who matters leaves us. Loss always brings change. Loss always brings change.

Adoption is a positive change that brings joy beyond words, and it also carries unimaginable loss and grief. Cali, I have watched you manage being adopted, relinquished by your biological parents, and leaving your homeland at such an early age with a fierce determination to learn and grow and be your best. Once a brown-eyed infant, innocent and hidden in a patch of tall grass near a Chinese factory for someone to find, you must have felt terrified as the sky darkened and your stomach felt empty and there was nothing but nature to protect you. You once said God and the animals surrounded you, and that image gave you great comfort. From an early age, you have had to form and flex spiritual muscles to create an uplifting story that explains your life and builds resilience whenever loss shows up. When I think of your life circumstances, Cali, I think of you recognizing that one of the most difficult choices is loving someone enough to let them go. How could a child learn that? Not only was your survival a miracle, but your parents' sacrifice brought us an answered prayer. Cali, your loss and theirs meant that we became parents and the three of us a forever family. We are forever grateful to your parents for the choice they made, and we remain reverent in our acknowledgment of how devastatingly difficult it must have been for them. .

And you, John, that vivacious five-year-old standing by the screen door of your cottage, anticipating your father's familiar loving eyes and the big arms that would lift you off the floor, leaving you screeching with glee on his return from the Nantucket Airport. Instead, your mother walked in alone much later than usual, calmly bent down to your bewildered face, and said, "Your father will never come home again." I can only imagine your heart closing down in that moment, starting to build a protective emotional barrier for yourself that took years and a pushy grief therapist to open. Your persistent purpose-driven path to face your grief has made you an empathic counselor, transforming your loss into a vocation to lead many others to manage their life's changes. That plane crash became a catalyst for giving from your pain and supporting many people.

The opposite of loss is not gain; it is growth. It is the effort made to reach inside, experience our grief, learn what is most important to us, and live on by transforming life's greatest challenges into opportunities to become more compassionate, wise, caring individuals. Learning how to rise to the challenge of change after loss is the greatest catalyst for growth and gives us the highest potential for living a meaningful and fulfilling life.

Cali and John, your lives exemplify this. Watching you both manage the daily and collective effects of loss with determination to learn and grow inspires me every day. It is not easy to grow resilient spiritual muscles, but the choice to try is the place to start.

I hope that every reader will become aware of their own experiences with loss and change and pass on their loss lessons to their sweet ones.

ACKNOWLEDGMENTS

Thank you to all the animals that showed up at various times to offer ideas, metaphors, and lessons, including the eagles, geese, whales, seals, deer, coyotes, rabbits, dogs, and cats, and all the other many ways nature inspired me. I am grateful.

Thank you to everyone mentioned in this book for your contributions to my learning and growing into myself. My parents taught us that we could never say thank you enough, so here is my small token of appreciation for so many people!

Thank you so much to the talented photographer of this cover, Sarah Quinn, for sharing this inspiring and uplifting photo of Cali.

To Kay Y, Radetta N, Nancy N, Pat E., and Roberta W., thank you for not only being female role models but also nurturing and encouraging me as my "EXTRA MOTHERS!" Thank you to my Vermont friends, my school friends, and my church friends, whom I think of with a smile, remembering a whole lot of fun!

To Bob Y, Rev, Professors Merle Jordan, Geoff Law, and Tom Tracy, thank you for introducing me to how faith can guide good men.

Thank you to Sarah W., Dottie, Cathryn, Timolin, and Casey for my growing years at prep school. You all taught me so much, and we had some great times together!

Thank you to my Batesie friends, who bestowed on me one of my greatest honors, the Alumni Community Service Award. No acknowledgment of my work has ever meant more.

Thank you to the people of Jason's community, who welcomed me with my lofty ideas and loved me through a tough transition. I will always love my time with all of you, especially the youth who have grown into such incredible people!

To Katie G. and Jason's family, thank you for honoring me with a journey that bound us together for life.

To Greg B., Gary A., and Mary Lee W., the original founders of the Jason Program, and Shelley M., Dick T., and all who came after them. To anyone who supported us with even a moment of your time and resources, thank you! That time in my life, and all of you, will forever hold a special place in my heart for your contributions and the very precious memories we created.

To all the luminaries who are mentioned in this book, whose light shone so brightly through their living unto death, and to their families, thank you for allowing me to walk beside you.

To my Team Katie coaches and teachers Marsha S., Allison C., Sue B., and Brianna B., thank you for all the hours of wisdom imparted and for encouraging me through many of my re-creations!

Thank you also...

To my business colleagues who have worked tirelessly to bring this book into the public eye, and to Terra P., Mariya V., Kat B., Kelly S., Kim L., and others who have contributed to my ability to find my voice, develop my skills, and bring my passion to the world.

To my Ukrainian friends Alexandra, Inna, Katya, and the women of The Soul. You inspire me every single day with your courage and compassion.

To the members of the Elisabeth Kübler-Ross Foundation Board and Advisory Board and the volunteers who have graced my life with their knowledge and supported me in continuing to honor her important contributions.

To Ken Ross, my "work brother," who trusted me when I wanted to bring his mother to Maine and continues to be supportive of my honoring her work with every hour of my day. Thank you, Ken, for your belief in me and for all the work you have done that has blessed all of us who continue your mother's work.

To Elisabeth Kübler-Ross, who for some reason saw in me someone who could impart her ideas and engendered in me a passion to follow her example. She is a guardian angel who often taps me on the shoulder and speaks her truth!

To my friends, my girl tribe, and their families, who have grown over the years, and Marie S., my bestie for over 55 years, who never once stopped believing in me and my passions!

A special thank you to the Marshalls and the Hills for being "chosen family!"

To Karen Y., Jaymie C., Svenja M., Heather M., Leah Y., Julie W., Michelle R., Lisa J., Stephanie M., Lisa G, Allison P., Mel R., and Maureen B. All of you have at various times lifted me up in diverse ways when I needed you and have always shared the best part of a girl tribe: love and laughter!

Thank you to my readers, Silja S., Heather M., Michelle D., Melissa B., Roberta W. and Yvonne V., for taking the time to read my manuscript and offer your suggestions!

To Cynthia A. for bringing us to Anacortes! To Joe and Billie and our many neighbors who have welcomed and supported us here.

To my editor, Chris, wow, what a ride… thank you for your many hours of support and tireless effort to bring my words into this form. You have been a gem to work with. Thank you! To Mary Beth Conlee, who became the proofreader and brought this book to its conclusion.

To our Italian daughter, Giulia, and her family, for being our European chosen family.

To my family, my nieces, their spouses, and their children: you are impressive people, and I am proud to call you family.

To my brothers, Ron and Randy: thank you for years of raising me to be the little sister you can be proud of.

To my parents and grandparents and to Phoebe and others who are gone too soon: thank you for supporting me in a way that empowered me to be effective. I am forever grateful.

To my sweet ones, John, and Cali, who have nudged me throughout my career to follow my passion and especially encouraged me to write this book. You both uplift me more than anyone else! You are my heart. Thank you.

§

A conversation between Austin, eight years old and dying of cancer, and his mother:

— Mom?
— Yes, what's up, Bud?
— I have something to tell you, and I hope you tell everyone in the world because it is important.
— What is it?
— There is love inside all of us and around all of us. The entire world is loving you! There are angels everywhere. They are the same on earth and in Heaven. And the purpose of life is to make a difference.
— Austin, how did you know that, and I didn't?
— You knew it, Mom, when you were little, but you forgot it when you grew up!

§

INTRODUCTION

United in stillness, we gathered around the motionless goose. Strangers drawn together, we somehow understood that we had a purpose. In silent reverie, we formed a circle around this motionless creature on the beach. It must have been minutes we stood in that sacred circle until out of the bright azure-colored sky came a magnificent flock. They flew in their v formation right towards us and hovered over him, offering him their wind, their support. Suddenly, he moved: a twitch… and then his wings began to flap, and with the aid of his flock, he began to rise. He faltered a few times, and we humans watching this miracle of nature became cheering onlookers as we witnessed him UPLIFTING and becoming once again a part of his winged family. No longer stricken, no longer defeated, he disappeared with them into the sky.

When one decides to author a book and your lifelong mentor is Dr. Elisabeth Kübler-Ross, the famous creator of the Five Stages of Grief* and the Kübler-Ross Change Curve*, there's no doubt that loss and change will be the primary themes. I learned from Elisabeth that how we understand and respond to loss and change has everything to do with how we live. Her greatest teachers happened to have been dying patients. Many of mine were as well, but like Elisabeth, I also learned from living, healthy very much alive people of all ages.

From the time I was a teenager, I began to compile my life's lessons. I have written my musings on sheets of paper, in journals, and in the margins of my client notes as a therapist. These pieces of wisdom have guided me to live my life awakened to whatever I can learn to make today better than yesterday. Now, these mental health musings are themes to the stories of my life and others who have shown me how to embrace a philosophy: *life's challenges offer us the opportunity to lift ourselves up, choosing to adapt to the changes and ultimately learn from the losses to become a better, more compassionate version of ourselves.*

From everyday changes to the hellish, tragic, insurmountable times that bring us to our knees, loss is a time when we can develop spiritual muscles. If we listen to messages that come in many forms from diverse sources, we can discover our capacity to lift ourselves up, face our loss, and emerge stronger and wiser than we were.

Each of the stories and themes in this book reflects this process of re-creating ourselves from loss. Listening during loss, taking a deep dive into our emotions, and identifying what and who we value can be the greatest gift we give ourselves.

This book and my mental health musings are based on the idea that we all *can* choose to live our lives taking baby steps towards building stronger more meaningful relationships with ourselves and all living beings around us *if we listen to the messages that come from loss.*

Throughout my life, both personally and professionally as a medical social worker, life coach, and licensed psychotherapist, I have witnessed people of all ages and stages re-creating their lives after crises exploded their sense of security and wholeness and sent them picking up the pieces of a new identity. Many of those I counseled were dying children and their families. Others were blind children, homeless teens, and the elderly fighting mental illness, to name a few.

You will read their stories in this book. You will see how they were shaken to their core by their circumstances. For many, the despair was so great it brought them to their knees. And yet somehow they made a choice to alter their course—to approach their obstacles by flexing their spiritual muscles and finding the means to triumph despite their challenges—even if the loss was their impending death.

Each found a way to redefine, refine, and restore their identity. This process—what I now call re-creation—began with a first uplifting step when some message coming from deep within caused them to make a courageous shift. Whether suffering the effects of a life-limiting illness, a premature birth, blindness, bereavement, or being unhoused, they found within themselves what Camus identified as the "invincible summer."

After years of recognizing and being inspired by the phenomenon of how even the tiniest of infants can harness this capacity, I began to understand that the common thread in my work was *loss, change,* and *growth.* Some event or circumstance denied the individual what they expected, what they wanted, or what they longed for, and this meant that somehow they had to re-discover a pathway they had never imagined.

My mother read Robert Frost to me from the time I was able to understand the poem "The Road Less Taken." She was trying to instill in me that no matter the circumstances, there is a time when we can pivot and consciously choose to discover potential and possibility, and that makes "all the difference."

Little did I know how much my mother's effort to teach me this vital lesson would shape not just my life but the hundreds of lives I have encountered personally and professionally. Those I counsel are often battling a challenge they feel they cannot overcome. I say to them, "What *can* you do?"

As the story of the stricken goose shows, even nature understands and exhibits the UPLIFTING way, built on the belief that when we feel broken, compassion can lift us to a higher place. In a state of woundedness, when we are vulnerable and at times stilted by something or someone who is taken from us, another comes along and offers us a way. If we pay attention to our life's teachers—who come in all ages and stages, human and animal—we can witness this miraculous dynamic throughout our lives. Loss offers us opportunities. When we are aware of that, we can make choices to learn life lessons and lift ourselves up. This in turn gives us the will and energy to lift up others.

To live an uplifting life is to rise to the challenge of change by learning from loss and growing more knowledgeable about how you as an individual can live a more fulfilling and meaningful life.

My dear friend Patsy taught me this lesson after the death of her eight-year-old son. She described her choice to make peace with grief as her friend, knowing it would come and go for the rest of her life. When it comes, she fully experiences all the dimensions of pain and listens to her longings. Patsy and her husband Rob are two of the most vital beings I have ever met because when they want to do something, they jump in and figure out how they *can* do it. They are also the most giving people because they transformed and re-directed their pain, as do many bereaved parents, into a non-profit to support families with seriously ill children. They epitomize the UPLIFTING way. For them, loss was a catalyst for growth.

Seven-year-old Katya, living in Ukraine with the threat of bombs falling and constantly fearing death, asked me how she could discover hope. Never have I been so challenged for a response until I remembered the stories in this book, and a still, small voice within me whispered: "Tell her to imagine her life as it will be!" Katya is an artist with great imagination, and I asked her to create the life she will someday live. She lit up and began making colorful images of paper dolls wearing the latest fashion outfits she longed to wear. She drew a house with a cat perched on the couch, just as she imagined it would be when she once again lives free of war.

One of the most traumatic moments for Katya was having to leave her beloved cat behind in Bucha when she fled the bombings. Longing for animal companionship, we brainstormed how she might borrow other people's animals until she could once again have her own. She began walking a dog to the nearby playground, allowing herself to believe that she might again feel safe enough to venture outside the four walls of her apartment and attend school. She began to meet friends, returned to gymnastics, and slowly, despite the danger surrounding her, she began to choose hope every day.

Each story in this book exemplifies uplifting bravery. The individuals described discovered an internal spirit, an explicable courage to rise out of misery and despair from their losses and choose change. Not just changes for themselves; by inspiring others, they impacted their community and made a difference. The ripple of compassion that emanated from their lives changed me and many around them. Their life lessons, messages, and modeling of how to live amid their trials are the motivation for my writing this book. Their stories need to be shared. Hundreds of lives have been impacted by these individuals. For all who know and knew them, they offer a deeper appreciation for life, love, and living.

What can be learned from their stories? Loss, defined as anything altering what we choose for our lives, is at the heart of each of their challenges. This may be experienced as tangible losses—loss of physical and mental abilities, loss of a home, loss of relationships, loss of loved ones, even the impending loss of one's own life or intangible losses that come from being unhoused or mentally ill, such as the loss of security, stability, or safety.

Their challenges served as catalysts for their growth into what they viewed as better or more authentic versions of themselves. They learned to leverage loss and champion change by both consciously or unconsciously choosing to reflect, reassess, redefine, and recreate some or many aspects of their lives. How? They listened. There was a choice point when they took time to address their mental, physical, emotional, and spiritual messages and change their mindset. They lifted themselves up!

A conscious commitment to the UPLIFTING way views each loss, large or small, tangible or intangible, as an opportunity to learn how to be more authentically kind. This path gains wisdom to live each day more compassionately.

It is not easy. Grief is a complicated, complex, and highly personal process unique to everyone. Asking yourself important questions can support you in developing your own approach to loss and grief. At the end of each chapter, you will find reflection questions based on my Re-Create model of loss, change, and growth. These prompts, specifically designed to guide you through your self-awareness and change process, are the foundation of learning to move from loss to growth. You may find yourself passing through various phases at different times. You can download additional information and a helpful guide on my website www.drkatieeastman.com Take time to reflect on your disappointments and change challenges, and allow this book to be part of your personal growth. Commit to the UPLIFTING way. Develop your own emotional toolkit, and discover within you a light that can lead you through the darkest of times.

Retreat · Evaluate · Clarify · Respond · Explore · Accept · Turn · Evolve

DR. KATIE EASTMAN

§

He is circling above the calm water. I see his majestic wings spread as he glides carefully and thoughtfully over the place where he wants to enter, but he hesitates. His white head tells me he is using his eagle eye to select just the right time to take the dive. He won't circle for long because he knows that his survival depends on entering that vast unknown to secure what he needs.

Like the eagle, we, too, make life choices. Our relationship to loss and our willingness to dive into the despair that sometimes lurks beneath the surface can be tenuous—unlike the eagle, who lunges toward what is hiding under the water's surface with determined precision. For us, taking the dive means uncovering the pain hiding under layers of accumulated losses we never healed from because we circled them instead of diving into the area of loss enough to experience the full extent of our pain.

Every painful experience leaves emotional and sometimes physical scars. In a sense, every loss leaves scar tissue. When we get into a tug of war about a situation, frustrated and angry that it shouldn't have happened, we thicken the scar tissue. Focusing on the event—not the opportunity to learn to make changes and grow in our life—is to focus on the wound and not the healing. When we allow a situation to be what it is without judgment and shine a light on the scar, we liberate that layer of loss. This empowers us with spiritual muscles of clarity, understanding, and a deeper love for self and others.

Sometimes softly and gracefully, and other times with gut-wrenching pain, I believe grief is there to release our scars and physically and metaphorically build new cells, new hope, and new life. It is hard to overcome our human need to judge, question, and resent what happens in our lives that produces deep loss. Yet, it is an essential process in re-creating our lives and choosing to truly live. It is our human metamorphosis.

Re-creating ourselves—making conscious choices about how we will face demanding situations, learn from them, and emerge transformed—is a process we can witness in each of the stories in this book. From these powerful examples of ordinary people facing hurdles and hardships, we can all learn how to build our internal resources to manage the inevitable large or small losses that will come our way.

Each of the people mentioned, including myself, found a way to rise up from a challenging situation by:

1. Identifying the loss, disappointment, and what they wanted to be different
2. Identifying what and or who they valued the most
3. Choosing to change their perspective from *can't* to *can*!
4. Making a difference by exemplifying a caring and compassionate approach to make change for others.

In this book, you will meet Jason, who, when diagnosed with cancer at fifteen years old, consciously chose to inspire others with his courageous example. Max, despite becoming blind at age eight, learned to swim. Michaela's indomitable spirit pushed her to crawl through the hallways of her school to her refuge in the library. You will also meet heroines like Elaina and MJ, whose children died and whose pain inspired them to create legacy projects to support others.

I did not understand until I authored this book that my own life story is filled with these same kinds of choices after loss that enabled me to change, evolve, and be ready to meet and embrace these wise individuals, who range in age from a premature infant to an eighty-year-old woman.

Learning to hold back our emotions prevents us from learning how to empathize. If you cannot recognize your own feelings, it's difficult to understand how someone else is experiencing something. As a social worker, I have held the hands of the dying, sat in the tiniest, filthiest homes, walked with destitute teens living on the streets, listened to the desperate attempts of child sexual abusers to stop abusing their children—no matter who or what the circumstances, remaining vulnerable and empathically available to their emotions and experiences without judgment or protecting my own feelings has been a constant challenge. In writing this book and acknowledging my own way of learning from loss, I recognized it was my willingness to choose to experience the impact of these changes that had the greatest influence on my ability to create a deeply meaningful life. These teachers and their stories inspired me to "feel to heal!"

In allowing ourselves to be guided by the powerful, subtle, and vital force that emanates from somewhere beyond our thoughts, we discover the magical, mystical reality of what I and others in this book have experienced. After thirty-five years of hearing others describe these moments and experiencing re-creations throughout my life, what I have come to understand is that this cycle of loss, change, and growth is foundational to living life to its fullest!

I invite you to the promise of an UPLIFTING life.

PART 1

THE FIRST LUMINARY

His mother carefully picked up the extension. Back then we didn't have cell phones, only dial-up receivers in different parts of the house, enabling eavesdropping on someone else's conversation. In this case, we felt it was highly justified. After all, how often does a household member receive a call from one of the most prominent women in the world? My friend Ellen Kingsley, a documentary film producer, had worked with this celebrated individual in Baltimore and arranged the call. Many well-known people had, at Ellen's request, made what they thought were supportive calls to Jason DeBusk, then nineteen years old and dying of cancer. A Vice President had chatted about football, and a famous Houston Oiler had told him to keep fighting. Many well-meaning individuals reassured him he would "beat this thing." Although he was appreciative of all the calls, Jason felt uneasy about the fact that none of them had authentically acknowledged the truth that Jason was likely dying.

This call was turning out very differently. This female icon took a deep breath and told him that he had lived a good life, more so than most people. She went on to reassure him with a phrase that resonated with me so deeply that I felt like my life stood still in the moment she shared the words: *Jason, the purpose of life is to make a difference, and you already have.*

We listened as Jason replied to her, "Thank you, that means a lot to me because that's what I wanted to do." The call ended shortly after, but for me, this phrase, this call, and this concept were about to lift my life to a new level. Why? It became the central belief at the core of my motivation from then on. Immediately, Jason and his wisdom and life example became my highest purpose. I was going to make a difference by telling his story. As I moved forward, Jason and his wisdom would guide me to many more teachers, many of whose stories are in this book.

CHAPTER 1

"IT'S NOT COURAGE, IT'S HAVE TO"

This major teaching hospital was a place where miracles were performed. As I began my internship, I knew I would be working with the best of the best. One morning, I entered this mecca of healing and hurried past dark-suited dignitaries with their visitor badges standing by the front desk. I was meeting my first patient today, and I was late! I rushed to get into the elevator, and when it finally reached the fourth floor, I flew out the door and into a small office. My supervisor was seated at her large metal desk flanked by a strapping, curly-haired redhead with an infectious smile. Wearing blue jeans and a T-shirt with the name of his high school football team on it, he was leaning back against the desk, his long legs sprawled out into half the room.

I seated myself in a comfortable leather chair in the corner, and my supervisor introduced me. "Mrs. Ryder, this is Jason. He will be your new patient. He has been assigned to the adult unit from the pediatric unit because of his age."

"I'm seventeen, almost eighteen. I have practice in an hour, so I need to make this quick. Who are you?" Jason asked.

"I'm a social worker. It's nice to meet you, Jason," I replied.

"You too, Ma'am."

"Oh, you don't need to call me ma'am. Mrs. Ryder or Katie is just fine."

Jason said, "Well, my ma says we show respect that way. So if you don't mind, she would get pretty upset if I didn't call you ma'am."

"OK. Whatever makes you comfortable."

"You sound different. You aren't from around here, are you?" he said.

"No, I'm actually from New England. I just moved here."

"Well, that explains the accent and not wanting to be called ma'am. You're from far away. I was born in Boston, though, so you can't be that bad for an Easterner."

"Jason," I heard my supervisor interject, "Mrs. Ryder will be working with you and your family during this next round of treatments. She's a student here, working with the brain tumor clinic, and she will be closely supervised. If you need anything, you know I'm always here."

"Does she know?" he asked.

"Know?" my supervisor said.

"About the new tumors? And the news that Dr. Paul gave me. No way I'm going to die in the next three months. I don't know what my doc was smoking when he read that test."

My mouth went dry. I was unable to speak. My thoughts raced back to my textbook—the page on how to speak to a dying person. My knees were shaking and my jaw tightening. I can't remember what it said. *I'm stuck! OK,* I thought to myself, *I am just going to try and relax and just be me.* I said, "Jason, I look forward to getting to know you better."

"OK. I sure have a lot to teach you!"

Something stirred in my stomach, and I took a deep breath. I didn't know where it was coming from, but I heard the words, *"Write down everything he says because someday you will tell his story."* Looking around for the human who might have uttered these words, I saw a file cabinet, my supervisor, and no one else. The voice was as clear as the water in the glass sitting on my supervisor's desk. And yet... where did it come from? I decided to believe it. At that moment, I began to take notes on my every encounter with this dying seventeen-year-old.

The next week was busy with orientation and meeting patients as they entered the hospital, learning as much about them and their families as I possibly could while they sat in the waiting area. The waiting area was a relatively small room with about twenty chairs lined up facing a television. My assigned patients were a captive audience. I decided it made sense to find Jason the next time he came to the clinic and speak with him.

Close to 3:00 p.m. on a Tuesday, I entered the clinic waiting area, said hello to the nurses at the check-in desk, and looked across the room for flaming red curls. There he was, sitting right in front of *Family Feud*, an adult on either side of him. One was a well-coiffed heavy-set blonde woman with beautiful red nails and matching lipstick. The other was a lanky man dressed in a T-shirt and jeans with a tense brow I could barely see. He was quietly reading a magazine.

"Hello, Jason," I greeted him.

He continued to stare at the TV but acknowledged my greeting. "Hello."

"How are you today?" I asked.

"Fine." His eyes remained fixed on the TV. "Mom," he said, "I've got this one. It's Kansas."

"I bet you're right, Son."

I tried to relaunch the conversation. "So, Jason, I've looked over your file, and what I've read must be incredibly challenging for you and your family." I noticed his face redden and his jaw tighten. He shifted his weight so his body was now facing away from me and completely in the direction of the TV.

Suddenly, he cheered, "Hey! I got it! It *is* Kansas!"

His mother, recognizing a young social worker drowning in Communication 101, gestured for me to sit down. She pointed to the TV as if to say *pay attention!*

I decided to listen to her and sit quietly. I joined Jason where he was at that moment, entranced by a TV show that was a great escape for him. Still and silent, I watched and waited.

Finally, he spoke. "Hey, do you watch this? It's my favorite show. I love the contestants. They are hilarious when they give some of their dumb answers. I like to outthink them!"

I stopped and pondered my response. "I really don't get much of a chance to watch TV these days, but I'm OK just sitting here for a bit until you go into your appointment."

The show went on for another thirty minutes until I heard the name *Debusk* called out. Jason suddenly tensed his muscles, took a deep breath, sat back in his chair, and stated, "Here goes nothing."

I decided to speak more with the attending nurse, who had known Jason for the five years he had been coming here since his Ewing's sarcoma diagnosis. Fran, a petite, fiery woman, explained how Jason had found a lump on his knee when he was fourteen—the first day of football practice. He was diagnosed a week later. He made the choice not to amputate then, but here he was, five years later. The cancer was back. And this time it had spread. Doctors were telling him he had only months left to live.

As she spoke, I felt the air rush out of my stomach. I became light-headed and unsteady on my feet. I sat down in a chair nearby and took a long, deep sigh. A few months? And *me* his social worker? What did I know about how to support a family who was going to lose their star athlete child? Larger-than-life Jason, who makes deals with the other patients so he can go first when he has practice. Jason the charmer, who bats his twinkling eyes and the entire nurse's station begins to flutter. Dead in a few months?

The next day, my conversation with Fran and the revelation of Jason's true prognosis were still ringing in my head. I stumbled past the cafeteria toward the chemo clinic, smelling the aroma of stale coffee combined with an antiseptic odor escaping from the clean rooms. I breathed in the refreshing scent of the fresh flowers on the stand outside the clinic. I opened the cold metal door and saw Jason in front of me with tubes in his arms, an IV pole beside him, and his mother sewing meticulous small stitches in a square, likely for a quilt to be placed on an oversized leather chair.

I greeted him with a "Hello, Jason," and saw him quickly pretend to sleep. He dropped his head, closed his eyes, and became still, his head hanging over the chair. *Hmm*, I thought to myself, *why would he pretend to be asleep? What am I doing to cause him to want to avoid me?* I decided to be direct. "Jason, I know you are not sleeping. Why are you pretending? Have I offended you somehow?"

He lifted his head, his cheeks flushed, his eyes narrowed, and he yelled, *"Your death questions really get on my nerves!"*

I felt as if I had been struck. Stepping back, I moved to the back of the room, where doctors were consulting with patients, and nurses and attendants with multi-colored scrubs were moving IV poles back and forth and fluffing up soft pillows for the new arrivals. The smell of fresh blood passing from the vein of each patient into the vials for lab results was making my stomach curl. I watched person after person take their turn to sit quietly in a high-back leather chair—a chair that was large and yet in some way subtle compared to the harsh brightness and the buzz of activity that surrounded it. It was a chair oversized enough for someone to get lost in.

I wanted to get lost at that moment. I wanted to retreat. I wanted to run back home. I wanted to flee to Vermont, to run back to the familiar. How did I get here? How did I offend my first patient in my first week?

It was the thought of Vermont that saved me. I thought of hours spent climbing the steep faces of the Green Mountains all by myself. I remembered when my grip would loosen and I would stop, take a deep breath, and find another rock to grab and another crevice to hold my foot. Then I would keep going. Was this any different? Comparing my work in oncology to climbing a mountain, I decided to regain my footing, stabilize, and rethink my way of communicating. When I had relaxed my body and settled my thoughts, I moved back to where I could see Jason and his mother. He was now pale, his face drawn, probably from the chemo. A bucket was placed beside him. Seeing my return, his mother's eyes widened. She lurched forward in her chair and said, *"Now is not the time."*

"Please," I said, in a small, barely audible voice, *"please, may I just apologize?"*

She must have seen my tears welling up. She reached out her hand ever so gently, touched my arm, and nodded her head towards Jason.

I walked slowly towards him. His arm was sitting on top of the arm of the chair with the needle protruding. His other arm was hanging off the other side. His head was leaning into the back cushion, his face long, his eyes sullen. He reminded me of the pieta and the sorrowful look of the mother holding her child.

I took a breath and started speaking. "Jason, I am new to this. I'm a student, I'm here to learn, and I am so, so sorry if I did anything or said anything to make this harder for you."

His IV began to beep, and a nurse quickly stepped in, switched bags, and pushed the necessary buttons. Watching the nurse and remaining silent, I waited for Jason's response.

He shook his head and said, "Talk to me like a friend. Walk beside me. Do what I do, don't tell me what I already know. And for God's sake don't be like every other adult who is constantly preaching to me! I know what's happening, and I refuse to give up. I am not going to die, and if I am, then I figure I will know it. Are you up for that?"

I shuffled my feet and took a few breaths before stating in a loud voice: "*Teach me!*"

His smile widened. He moved forward and extended one long arm to me, and we shook hands. And there, with the moans and the groans of the people in those black chairs and the scurrying of the professionals intermingling with the patients, we became teacher and student. The lessons that I would learn from this greatest of my luminaries resonate with me to this day.

Never give up.
Keep a positive attitude.
Communicate honestly.
Don't be afraid to cry.
Trust God.
Don't worry.
Be a friend to all.
Embrace life.
Make a difference.

That same inner voice that had told me to write down everything Jason said kicked in at that moment, and I felt a sudden urge to invite Jason to come and speak to the youth group at my church about his experience with cancer. Jason gathered strength from helping others. He seemed to become energized and motivated by a sense of purpose. He frequently visited pediatric cancer patients and their families to offer support.

I had an instinct that sharing his wisdom and teaching not just myself but others what he was learning about life with cancer might give him a reason to live. His immediate response validated my thoughts. "I would love that!" He sat up with infectious energy, and in that moment, he named me his agent.

This initial speaking engagement led to many others. Jason seemed to thrive from sharing his message of hope with various groups of people, including groups from many different faiths—Jewish, Muslim, Christian. He was enthusiastic about his new passion. His speeches were inspirational testimonies of how his Mormon beliefs helped him cope with his disease. Jason was able to attribute meaning to his experience and incorporate this meaning into all aspects of his life. His initial speech to my youth group began a series of speeches that led to the book he was to write with me about how to cope with problems in life.

Jason began to use the phrase "Never, never, never, never, never give up." I told him that I had found out that Winston Churchill originated its use, but Jason's reply to this was, "He's dead. Now it's my turn." This became a motto he often shared with others who were feeling down and defeated. He was upbeat and encouraging to other children suffering the effects of cancer in ways that seemed to brighten their world.

Jason's speeches had a great impact on many people. He encouraged other adolescents to stop using drugs. He asked that any who had contemplated suicide come talk to him because of how important it is to keep living no matter what happens. One of my favorite examples of his impact on others is a story about a young man who, having heard Jason speak about coping with cancer, entered a drug rehabilitation hospital to quit drinking. He stated about this choice, "If Jason could do what he did, I can quit drinking."

Another important aspect of Jason's feeling of purpose was his relationship with younger kids who had cancer. Jason's work at a cancer camp held each summer was a great source of personal pride for him. When he first arrived at the camp, the younger boys were all wearing hats. Arriving hatless with his bald head showing, he exclaimed, "What are you all wearing hats for?" With Jason's example, they took their hats off and were helped to come to terms with their baldness.

In addition to his camp relationships, on occasion Jason was introduced to other cancer patients at the hospital. With permission from parents and members of both care teams, I introduced him to a blind amputee patient. This eleven-year-old was depressed, and none of the medical staff had been able to reach him. My hope was that Jason's humor and sensitivity might be helpful. It was amazing how his easy-going approach facilitated an emotional opening up. The two of them would play Nintendo, and during the game, the boy would tell Jason how he was doing. They became fast friends.

Introducing these boys was an important decision for me.

Understanding the poor prognosis for each of them, I was presenting them with another eventual loss when one of them died. I made my decision to introduce them anyway based on my thinking that this was another way of introducing Jason to a sense of purpose while simultaneously providing the other boy with some needed peer support. This was a difficult dilemma. However, I decided, along with the parents and health professionals, that the improved quality of life might outweigh the risk. They helped each other until Jason became too sick to visit the young boy.

This was an example of what I came to understand from Jason and many other luminaries: it's not how long they lived, but how they lived. Jason lived until he died, offering his skills, gifts, and talents to others as long as he possibly could. His last speech was to over 1,000 youth who gave him a standing ovation. Frail and having just thrown up in the parking lot, he made his way to the podium and inspired everyone to live life differently.

While he lived before he died, Jason taught me and others perhaps the most unforgettable lesson of all: how facing the fear of dying of cancer at age 17 *was just necessary*. "It's not courage, it's have to," he explained.

Over time, I came to realize that teenagers are like Moses: they look out at the promised land of adulthood with matter-of-fact determination that it is right over the horizon. There is no room for contemplating death when facing a life-threatening condition; it's simply not important. There is fear, of course, but facing fear head-on and diving into life anyway is their approach. Some studies indicate that the size and development of a teenager's brain may have something to do with this deliberate lack of attention to fear and harm. Perhaps. Regardless, there is wisdom in approaching any difficult situation with this kind of tenacity. To feel the fear and do what you want to do anyway is a path through any challenge or obstacle.

This approach to living became the guiding principle of my life and my work. Think of those transition points in life when we choose changes that cause us to shift direction and seek something more, something better, something easier. "It's got to be better than this," we think. What gives us this courage to risk, to choose differently? These are questions I ask not only of myself but of those I work with. During times of loss and change, these queries can be the light that illuminates what is most important for us.

Jason knew. It's deeper than courage. It's deeper than choice. It is our human spirit that strives to be happy, to experience joy, and to smile like a little child playing on the beach. To live life to its fullest does not take just courage; it requires a willingness to be unwavering in our pursuit, to wake each day determined to make it better than the last. To live in this manner is to view our choices as "have to" because we are driven by a passion that allows us to do nothing else but to live! Like the tide that returns each day a bit differently than yesterday, we are meant to do the same. Jason understood this. Faced with death, he embraced every bit of life he could.

§

Recognizing that Jason's meaningful words could be lost after his death, I began to consider ways that he could preserve his thoughts and create a tangible legacy. We decided to write a book together. What you are reading now in this chapter and throughout this book is the result of a heartfelt promise I made to Jason that I would tell his story and create his legacy through my life's work.

My hope was that we could write the story together. Unfortunately, his disease progression made writing a difficult task, so instead, I organized a video project whereby he could tell his story before he died, preserving his words so that I could pass them on. His one wish had been to help others, and I felt that this video would be a way of fulfilling this wish.

Jason's words during the taping of this video were inspirational. I also did a personal interview with him, asking him to tell me what he wanted others to know. It was a powerful part of my saying goodbye to him. In a sense, it was coming full circle from the early days, when he told me my death questions were "getting on his nerves." The following is my interview with Jason and what he wanted all of us to know.

K: Who do you want this video to be for?

J: Anyone who thinks giving up is easier than going on with their own fight.

K: What is your goal for the video?

J: A learning experience for others to teach them how to go on.

K: Why do you want to make the video?

J: Telling others how I get through it through prayer and stories of faith and how maintaining a positive attitude helped me.

K: Did you ever feel insecure?

J: No, I didn't allow the cancer to change me, I had to grow up faster and I took less for granted.

K: What do you mean, "not taking life for granted"?

J: Life is worth a lot more than people think it is. When life comes to the point where it may stop, you take it less for granted.

K: What about the idea that you may die?

J: It's there, but you don't have to think about it if you have peace of mind; set it aside.

K: What is most helpful for you?

J: Saying "how are you" instead of "how are you feeling." People who aren't afraid to kiss and hug me.

K: What is least helpful?

J: People who ask questions about things they don't understand—making conversation out of their own discomfort, not getting beyond the small talk.

K: What do you want everyone to know?

J: Say what comes from the heart and persevere; personal interaction makes a difference.

One of my favorite memories of Jason is from a synagogue where he shared some of his wisdom. This professed Mormon had a message, and he brought it into many different settings. I remember him barely being able to stand in front of the group of Jewish teens and adults as he delivered a speech in which he urged them to never, never, never, never give up. He pointed to me with his then-bony finger and said that no matter what you are facing, there is someone who will believe in you and help you get the support you need. And then, in front of a circle of strangers, he exclaimed how much I, "Miss Katie," had helped him to live. Both of us were crying, and we exchanged a knowing look, sending a message into each other's eyes as if to say, "This is almost over and yet it is forever."

He with his t-shirt and jeans and bald head—barely able to walk, his speech slowing—and me with my beehive hairdo, big earrings, bright, long, hand-painted shirts, all the rage in my small town—were switching places. Soon, the student would have to become the teacher.

§

As Jason grew weaker, if any of us around him got down, *he* was the one to challenge us to "chill" more often, to enjoy life's challenges by having fun. He reminded me of this lesson at a painfully poignant moment just days before his death. His breathing was beginning to slow, a sign that he might be starting his transition towards death. Like most mothers do, Jason's mother was desperately trying to somehow send him her life energy to restore his own. As his breathing slowed, she would say, "Jason, breathe!" Repeatedly, as the space between breaths became longer, she would express with growing despair, "Jason, breathe!" Finally, perfectly on cue, this tiny, familiar voice spoke up: "Mom, breathe!" We laughed and cried at that moment, knowing full well that there was a time fast approaching when Jason would draw shorter breaths and eventually leave us.

§

I don't think anyone could have driven faster and safer than I did the morning Jason's mom notified me that the hospice nurse felt that Jason was dying imminently. As I raced from the university where I was continuing my master's degree in social work to Jason's home, normally a 90-minute drive, I found myself making a mental list of what I had rehearsed in my mind—what I would voice if given the chance to say goodbye. I decided to allow my heart to speak spontaneously in the moment, and turned my attention instead to the promise I made to his girlfriend Katie, who was already at Jason's home preparing to say goodbye. I remembered the poignant moment when, seated on the hood of my car, she had asked me when the day came that Jason was dying if I would go to the high school and pick up her sister to be with her when Jason took his last breath. I had planned with the school that whatever day I showed up, they would implement the grief response they had in place. My presence and Katie's sister leaving would signal that the dreaded day of Jason's death had come. It was all planned, and when I drove into the school parking lot, I half expected Katie's sister to be waiting.

Instead, I was met at the door by a teacher, a tall, intimidating man who raised his shoulder in defiance and stood at the front door demanding that I wait to enter the school because the students were taking tests. *Wait? Jason is dying now, we cannot wait!* I tried desperately to convey the urgency of getting Katie's sister out of class, but he refused to move aside and allow me to pass through the door that led to the classrooms. He wanted me to wait an hour until lunch. From somewhere within me came an irrepressible surge of adrenalin fueled by my grief and my promise to a teenage girl who was about to lose her best friend—militant at this point, remembering the many stories of people dismissing teenagers and minimizing their needs—and I forced myself past this man and broke through the door into the hall. I did not care who or what was in my way; I was on a mission. I found Katie's sister, and the minute she saw me, everyone knew. As we made our way out of the school, I never looked back, even though I could hear the sobbing, and I knew that my appearance meant there was now a school full of mourners behind me.

We got to Jason's home and found Katie and Jason's mother stroking his head and saying loving things to him. I bent down beside him and said, "Jason, I will not only tell your story. I will dedicate my life's work to you."

He was barely conscious at this point. I left his side, tears rolling down my face. Katie told him she loved him and stroked his head, and he died.

We surrounded him with a prayer circle shortly after—his family and chosen family, or special family, as I was named. It was a day I will never forget.

A few weeks later, I placed my foot on top of a large shovel as I dug past the dust into the soil below. Next to me was a granite headstone and bench with the words "Never Never Never Never Give Up" next to Jason's name and date of death. I placed the sapling of an oak tree, small, young, and fragile, into the place where it would grow and eventually cascade over Jason's resting spot. Nearby, on the road that backed up to his grave, the entire town—more than 1,000 people—had made a procession to remember him. Balloons had been sent into the heavens that day with messages saying, "Thank you for all you gave and taught us." As I painstakingly replaced the nurturing dirt that would protect the tiny oak, I wept, tears flowing for my friend, my teacher, my mentor, and someone who changed my life forever.

EPILOGUE: THE PROMISE

Here is an excerpt from my dissertation, "Looking through Both Sides of a Window: a work designed to offer a comprehensive model of care for adolescents dying of cancer." It's an interview I conducted with Jason before he died. He wanted to help others understand that they, too, could approach death with courage and "have to."

§

I am seated on a pale green, weathered couch with tan pillows covered with cat fur. The smell of kitty litter along with chocolate sheet cake baking in the oven wafts in the air. Jason, lying beside me with his head lifted by several fluffy down pillows, has a bowl beside his head just in case. The TV is on, as always, and we are watching a movie. Jason's girlfriend, a pixie, tomboy girl with dark hair, dark skin, and a rugged, powerful body, sits on the other side of him. She gets up to get some popcorn.

"Katie," Jason says in a very mellow tone, unusual for him. "This guy dies too, right?"

"Yes, Jason, he does."

"I wonder if he was scared when he was flying that plane into death."

"I don't think anyone wouldn't be scared when they are dying, Jason. But what do you think?"

"I think I am not ready, but I also know that if it comes, I will be OK. I have a lot of support. Thank you, Katie, for hanging in there with me, for being that friend I asked you to be."

I can feel my eyes watering, and I think about the cat playing in the corner to stop the tears.

"You're welcome, Jason. I'm here for however you need me."

"I know you are, and my parents need you too. Make sure they are ok. Promise me."

"I promise to try, Jason."

"And tell my story, Katie. You seem to know me and what I think and what's important to me. I want to inspire others. I have lived a lot longer than anyone thought, and I think it's because of how I think. Tell others, teach them like I taught you. OK?"

I reach for the crocheted comforter, gingerly placing the multi-colored squares over his now thin, wiry body.

He reaches out and high-fives me.

We know at that moment that we are joined in a lifetime partnership. It lasts past two years of treatments, the break-up of his three-year relationship, the state championship of his football team, and one month of attending college, only to have to return home from the increasing fatigue as his tumors grew. It lasts until today.

"It's not courage, Katie. It's have to."
I learned that and so much more from Jason.

REFLECTION QUESTIONS

1. Has anyone or anything inspired you to never give up?
2. What makes someone courageous?
3. When you think of living a meaningful life, what do you think of?

PART 2

MY LOSSES, TEACHERS, AND LIFE OF SERVICE

I have learned and relearned during times of loss and transition that there are love lights that appear when I need them. When I become aware that I need support and give voice to that need, either silently or aloud, gifts begin to appear like fireflies in the sky. And when my heart is breaking, I know that if I pay attention, I will see those glimmers of light—the gifts, the fireflies of hope and love—even during my darkest moments.

This book is filled with these gifts of love and hope—so many people, places, and signposts that led me to make choices and those "road less taken" leaps of faith that have made all the difference in my life. Maybe the indigenous folks have it right: We can hear the messages from that loving spirit whenever we are still enough to hear it and present enough to listen. Those messages don't have to come in a building or a religious gathering place; if we decide we want to hear them, we can hear them whenever and wherever we listen.

In this section, drawn from events in my life, each chapter ends with reflection questions such as these to help you think about the lessons of loss, love, and light in the story you've just read. After each story, I invite you to pause and ponder upon your own experiences of love and light and ask:

- What were the love messages in this story?
- Where did they come from?
- Did I listen?
- Where were the signposts and the love lights?

CHAPTER 2

LOOK FOR THE LIGHT AND THE LOVE

Where and when does loss begin?

My childhood experience supports the concept that early losses form how we see ourselves and who we are becoming. If only I had learned at an early age that my value had nothing to do with wearing a bikini or good grades! I needed, as do most children, to be reminded that my self-worth comes from inside. I, like you and your children, are valuable because we exist. We do not have to earn our preciousness. Yet if you ask a child over the age of eight to tell you what is most important and valuable about them, they will likely recount a certain accomplishment or describe their talents or be unable to answer—because they are blind to their inherent value.

§

Like most children, my earliest loss was self-esteem. Throughout my childhood, I battled with weight issues that led to years of merciless bullying. It began as early as five years old, when our family moved from suburbia, where we had neighbors a few feet away on all sides and families with kids all around us, to an isolated lakeside house with no one under the age of fifty anywhere to be seen. With no playmates or swing set, what can a five-year-old do on a beach alone? Well, unfortunately, the answer for me was to sit on a log eating snacks with my dog. Even at this early phase of my life, I was learning the fine art of numbing pain with food.

When I started school, my mother, attempting to give me a sense of belonging, threw me a swim party and invited my kindergarten class. This led to another mortifying moment. She had bought me a two-piece bathing suit, and just as I dove into the water, the strap broke, revealing my newly developing chubby frame to my supposed new friends. Being true-to-form five- and six-year-olds, they laughed at me, and my new nickname of "Fatty" was born. And Fatty was just one name. Heifer ("Heff" for short), fat girl, little fat one—these were just a few of the childhood nicknames that sent me rifling through my mother's purse to steal money for candy that I would secretly stash to soothe myself.

Food was my friend. It took away the pain of loneliness and feeling isolated. I could always count on a sugar rush from a Hershey bar to lift my mood. My eating and weight issues continued through elementary school. I would steal a $1 bill from my mother's purse every day, sneak away to the local store, and buy Reese's peanut butter cups that I would scarf during recess. The bullying, of course, continued as well. In elementary school, a group of classmates put glue on my chair so they could laugh when I stood up and split my pants.

Continuing throughout my school years, bullying and the resulting humiliation, sadness, and low self-esteem represented the first significant loss in my life.

But this is a book about how loss leads to change and growth, and one day, during an extreme bullying incident, I experienced the first glimmer of hope from an inner voice urging me to do something different. Although I hardly knew it at the time, the message from that inner voice would become a recurring theme of my life: *In the face of loss, send out light and love.*

I remember that day well. I had arrived late to the Y for their free swim. I became aware of that familiar smell, and my stomach began to churn with anticipation. Cheap perfume, that fruity, flowery nauseating smell that permeates the lockers of girls trying to be sexy, was the first thing I smelled as I moved past her. I saw her unkempt long brown hair and her halter top and tight-fitting pants snug against her almost anorexic body. As someone bustling to get by pushed against me, I fell in front of her—my nemesis, the person who was quick to call me fat or Heifer or any other description of an oversized object. Her locker door with its sharp gray edge made its way to my side. I called out in pain only to hear her laughter. The pain was sharp, and I knew the cut was deep, but not as much as the anguish I felt at once again being made to feel like half a person, small and insignificant, writhing in pain with no kind response. I could taste the phlegm in my throat gathering as I struggled to make a sound, and I felt myself getting dizzy. Oh no—when I fell into the locker, it caused the door to shut on her finger. By now a crowd had gathered, the gawking onlookers trying to be the first to discover what had happened to be able to spread the gossip.

I found myself sitting in the Director's office, and like most of you who have been bullied, I feared the fact that the secret was out in the open and that meant my mother would now know.

Sure enough, Mary Eastman came rushing into the office like a blue tornado, a flood of energy bombarding the Director with questions, demanding answers about who and what had caused this to happen. As she pushed me to describe the extent of the incident, the physical and mental anguish of the constant taunting got the best of me and I blurted out in detail the time my nemesis had put salt in my milk and when she and her friends passed notes about me that were "accidentally" passed on to me describing me as big and ugly, and multiple other incidents I have since chosen to repress and dismiss from my thoughts. I could hear my mother's gasps at the increasingly detailed retelling of these stories, and when I could finally take a deep breath, I knew what I had done. I had come clean, and this meant that the adults now knew the extent of what my experiences here had really been.

The irony of bullying is that the victim often fears other people knowing and retaliation more than the bullying itself. How we respond is related to our self-worth. In my case, I felt conflicted: I just wanted to maintain peace and contain the situation, but my mother let loose on the Director like a pit bull in the backyard, demanding that there be some sort of consequence for these unruly kids.

My greatest fear became a reality. My mother calling the mothers of these girls meant when I least expected, I would be the target of severe retribution, and I knew it. I had watched these girls in action and knew that they would harm me if given the chance. I took some time to consider how I could best manage if they tried to beat me up. Somehow, some voice inside my head told me to hold an image of light and love, flexing what I would later call my spiritual muscles: that immense power we have within us to overcome adversity. On that day, flexing my spiritual muscles meant maintaining a compassionate stance no matter what. Thinking of the lyrics to an old song we had learned when I was a little girl, "This Little Light of Mine," by Harry Dixon Loes, and reminding myself *I'm going to let it shine*, I decided I would sing that song to myself through the entire ordeal.

I walked out of the double doors and there they were, a gang of six vicious-looking girls ready to pounce. Taking a deep breath, I decided to hold an image of light in my mind and to believe I would be okay. I started walking, not even catching the eye of any of them, consciously taking each step with fake confidence and self-assurance. Although I wanted to throw up or run as fast as I could, I tried to lift my shoulders back and began singing to myself, *This little light of mine, I'm going to let it shine*. They followed me, taunting me with any insult they could muster. They came so close to my back that I could feel someone's breath on the nape of my neck. But I kept my body moving forward in a steady rhythm of calm. When we got past the corner store and onto the neighborhood street lined with houses, I thought for sure this would be their time to make a move, but still they just kept close, yelling obscenities and belittling me in any way they could. *This little light of mine, I'm going to let it shine*. When we turned onto my street, a rural road with barely a house to be seen, I was ready. I heard them reach into their pockets, and one by one, they started throwing rocks at me. Oddly, though, none of them were aimed at me directly. I heard each stone hitting the pavement and coming within inches of me for the half-mile it took to get to my driveway. Then they turned around and walked in the other direction. There was ample opportunity for them to hurt me in any way they chose to, but they didn't. Perhaps my ignoring them and not giving away my power made a difference? Running into my home, I threw myself on my bed and sobbed, barely able to breathe, my stomach still tied in a knot.

I have asked myself many times if holding on to an image of light made the difference in that bullying situation. Did my choice to keep sending the bullies light, to send them messages of love through my terror, even though I was certain they were going to harm me, work? Is there an energy we can send to another person that is not spoken but still received? Is there a way to exude compassion without words or action?

And if there is a powerful love that supersedes acts of violence, then why does it only work sometimes? Why are some people saved and others not? Why do mass shootings happen when people pray for them to stop? That is an existential question that I, like all of you, have no answers for. But I still want to ask the question because maybe, just maybe, it does work sometimes.

I wrote this book believing that if my philosophy and thoughts can change one situation for one person, then it is well worth it—then I will have made a difference. If there is one person who is in a bullying situation at work or home who can find the love of self to give them the strength to stand up to the bullies in their lives, to speak their truth, and to allow help to come, then that is one more person on earth with a deeper capacity for compassion, and telling my story was worth it.

After this event, I began to hold on to what I decided was true: sometimes, it *does* make a difference to believe that there is something beyond myself that can bring love into any situation. This idea, which first emerged on that terrifying afternoon, became the foundation for my understanding of how to consciously face any experience: look for love and the light for comfort. When my clients relay their stories—their "change challenges"—and their yearnings to face their losses, I repeat to them, "Look for the love and the light." In other words, beginning with yourself, listen for the messages that remind you unconditionally that you are worthy of the life you desire. Letting go of guilt or shame or blame will open you to receive the support you deserve.

This is why my philosophy is based on lifting and *lighting* yourself up—which, as you will see repeatedly in the stories of this book, will lead you to lifting and lighting others up. Although I hardly knew it on that terrifying afternoon, I had found a way to lift myself up: by sending out light.

How was I able to hear and follow that message that seemed to come from some kind of wise voice? Why did I listen? This was the first of several mystical experiences I would have in my life—love whispers when a voice from somewhere beyond me seemed to be sending a guiding message.

I believe my willingness and ability to hear that still, small voice has a lot to do with my contemplative time in nature. When we moved from suburbia to a lake when I was five years old, I found myself living in a summer playground... until summer ended, and people left the area. Suddenly, I was surrounded by deafening silence. With no one to play with, I had to learn to entertain myself. As I grew older, I passed my time reading *Anne of Green Gables*, a favorite classic by Lucy Maude Montgomery, and other books about female heroines. *Anne of Green Gables* inspired me to find my own Avonlea. I spent hours walking in the woods down a path that was once an old railroad track, flanked on one side by houses and Lake Champlain on the other. Following this long dirt trail into my wooded escape, I created a sacred place where I would perch on a log and listen to the subtle sounds of the whistling wind and the chickadees sweetly singing and the waves gently rubbing against the rocks. At times, this was my way of reconnecting with myself. When I felt the most misunderstood by family and friends, I found solace in the quiet of the woods and the water. It was there my heart could speak, my longings would reveal themselves, and I could escape into my fantasies of what life was meant to be. It was there I first began to contemplate, in *Anne of Green Gables* style, the importance of considering my actions in relation to a bigger world. The dreamer in me was born in this spot, and it was there, surrounded by Vermont maples and glistening green fir trees, that I had a sense that my life mattered. I learned from this conscious choice to discover the love and light in all my experiences and to pay attention and look for my enlightened teachers.

REFLECTION QUESTIONS

As you reflect on your early losses and messages of love and light.

1. What did you learn as a child about facing demanding situations?
2. Do you remember a moment when you felt threatened, criticized, or judged, and you could have maintained a compassionate attitude?
3. If you could teach your five-year-old and fifteen-year-old self about loving themselves, what would you tell them?

CHAPTER 3

THE CIRCLE OF CARE

"Look for the light" is a theme you will find running through this entire book. You can look for the light to help yourself and to help others. When you are lifting and lighting up others, you become part of their Circle of Care—the close-knit, caring community that helps those suffering from loss.

People who appear in our lives and become part of our Circle of Care can be mirrors reflecting who we want to be and how we might live our lives. They foster a sense that not only are we ok, but that we have something to offer others.

It was an unexpected but powerful circle of care that saved me from the bullying I had known my entire childhood and transformed me into someone who wanted to help others. One group of people who had the greatest influence over my life at this time began with a friendship to a bestie named Karen. We met in school and became fast friends, and she, along with her family, brought light and caring into my childhood.

This family had struggles they turned into blessings. One of their children, an especially able little guy named Rick, had one of the most infectious, joyful smiles I have ever seen. If you were having a difficult day, Rick was guaranteed to get you out of it. At times he required time and attention, but this family never ever gave the impression that caring for him was difficult. They took turns and shared him with those of us who were blessed to know them. Rick and the Youngs embodied the uplifting spirit.

The Youngs welcomed me into their family. There was no

teasing—well, at least none that left me feeling insecure, only accepted. And they introduced me to a new world, one where I discovered a safe place to be myself and find others who cared: church. Karen invited me to sing in the choir with her, and I did not just learn how to sing songs, I learned and discovered my voice. Not only could I carry a tune, but singing was to become one of my deepest forms of expression. Here was a place where I could fully engage my emotions. Unlike other places, where feeling deeply was considered a weakness, here it was embraced. For the first time, I felt understood and accepted.

The Youngs also introduced me to skiing. I had learned from years of ridicule to hate my body, and therefore myself, until Karen took me skiing. Her father was on the ski patrol, and we would head up to Madonna Mountain every Saturday and spend the day conquering our fear of heights, learning agility, and maneuvering over moguls by learning to place our poles to bounce off the edge of these raised mounds of snow and ice. We learned to increase our ability to take risks by daring to take jumps, which after a soaring take-off left a rush of adrenaline and a sense of invincibility. With this adventurous sport, I started to discover my physicality. Here on these snow-capped hills with my best friend, I was strong and capable, and at least temporarily, the words of the bullies left me.

At the time I was introduced to the Youngs and church, I was, like many children and teens, crying out for acceptance, for inclusion, for a group to bring me in and show me that I was ok. I desperately needed to belong—and, thankfully, my life changed because a loving friend and her family saw that, took me under their wings, and offered me the opportunity to become a part of them. Church also became a place where I found a community of friends who shared something with me: a commitment to care. The message of unconditional love that I received from this community as a struggling young girl swept me into the fold and taught me to love myself and others. That little light of mine shone brightly in the circle of care created by the church and the Youngs. It was there I also learned the value of, as Rilke said, loving the questions in life. Faith became a grounding force for good that lit me up when I needed it.

FAITH AND QUESTIONS

One of the greatest sources of strength for many of us is to hold a belief or faith that gives our lives meaning. It is important, however, to distinguish between religion and spirituality. We are all spiritual beings with spiritual beliefs. Whatever gives your life meaning and purpose, whatever gets you up in the morning and keeps you going, is your spiritual belief. Some choose to gather, share, and discover their beliefs with rituals and teachings prescribed by a religion. I am grateful to have found a way of believing and following the teachings of Christ that offer me a place to ask questions and seek my truth. I have never found answers without more questions, but the life and teachings of Christ are one of the most important sources I have to find both the answers and the questions they might raise. One might say that in church, I found a way to feel a universal connection to every living being. Love and light became my strongest voice and grounded me in acts of compassion.

As Rainer Maria Rilke wrote in his *Letters to a Young Poet*, "Be patient toward all that is unsolved in your heart and try to love the questions themselves, like locked rooms and like books that are now written in a very foreign tongue. Do not now seek the answers, which cannot be given you because you would not be able to live them. And the point is, to live everything."

IMAGINATIVE DISCOURSE

How often do we offer teenagers the opportunity to question what they are taught—to hold their own beliefs and challenge the ideas of their elders? One essential aspect of growing into an intellectually stimulating thinker is to learn how to engage in critical thinking and active discourse. Finding ways to introduce yourself and your children to this opportunity can assist you in opening your mind, expanding your worldview and your values, and providing new meaning to your faith.

Questioning and evaluating our beliefs is healthy, and I am so grateful that my church experience included a "spiritual boot camp." Our leader was our youth pastor, Reverend Nelson—a tall, tanned, athletic-looking

40-something adult with a smile that left you feeling like you were important to him. 'Rev' challenged us to question everything and encouraged us to think critically about how the Bible might have some helpful information. But what we loved most about Rev was that he never told us what to think; instead, he was one important adult in our lives who valued anything we said.

Interrobang was what we called this process of questioning, in which the end result was not an answer but an idea to consider that was designed to leave us deep in thought for days afterward. Interrobang led to some lively and meaningful discussions. My love of imaginative discourse began in that small room in the church parsonage, huddled over a cup of soup and surrounded by my peers. Rev became a strong teacher of the value of not just forming a belief but putting that belief into action.

FAITH AND PERSISTENCE

When I was fifteen, I had the privilege of climbing Longs Peak in the Rocky Mountains on a church youth group trip. Rev, who led the trip, warned us of the importance of watching our steps, taking it slowly, attending to our breath—and above all, we were told to support one another and work as a team.

Reminded that the air at this altitude might challenge some of us, we were taught the warning signs of altitude sickness and told to help each other navigate through the steeper sections. Leaving just after dawn, we began in plenty of time to reach the summit before the weather changed at midday. The adventure unfolded as several of our team members struggled with the altitude and had to stop. I'm not sure if it was the "Vermonter" in me, but I powered on.

Near the last section of the hike, the trail narrowed as we rounded a very steep corner, and the precipice caused me to feel sheer panic. There was barely room for a shoe, and as each of us admitted we were scared, we were talked through the tight passage with reassuring messages like:

- Others have made it through here.
- You can do it.

- Have faith.
- Go slowly and breathe through your fear.

One by one, we made it to the summit. Much to our surprise, after feeling we had accomplished such an amazing feat, we found many people at the top, sunning themselves and enjoying the view!

When I think of that day, I am reminded of those instructions: know that you can do something; have faith that what you need is there; and go slowly and breathe through your fear when you become insecure. Those principles were guiding lights, a beacon that led me through my teenage years. Back then, I was barely beginning to understand what loss meant. Amid a childhood marked with a sense of feeling lost and alone, accepting the Youngs as chosen family and responding to Reverend Nelson's teachings established the foundation for a life of service.

FAITH IN ACTION

YES—Youth Experience in Service—was the name of our church-sponsored mission trip to offer ourselves in service for ten days. Led by our beloved youth pastor, Rev, this group of fifteen- and sixteen-year-olds boarded the plane for Mexico with excitement.

When we arrived in Juarez, México, I was assigned a painting job. We were renovating a school building for an orphanage there. When we first arrived, the children gathered in a group and sang *This Little Light of Mine* in Spanish. My heart was so full, and I was determined to do the best painting job I could. However, I had never done this before, and had not factored in that when you paint above your head, the paint drips. So, within minutes of stepping up the ladder and rolling sky-blue paint on the thick adobe walls, my glasses were covered with dripping paint. Laughter ensued, and my nickname, "Bird," famous for her droppings, was born.

I could have been insulted and internalized the comments, but seeing the smiles of these cherub-like faces of children dressed in reds and pinks and orange and bright cheerful clothes singing to us in gratitude… well, I couldn't have cared less! Those kids and that experience of service were the beginning of my life as a social worker. On that trip, we also rebuilt homes destroyed by a flood in Big Thompson Canyon in Colorado and worked on a Navajo Reservation doing odd jobs. And everywhere we went, we were greeted with kind, compassionate gratitude and felt welcomed and needed. We were making a difference in the lives of people who were not born into the white privilege that I had been. Children in all these places had only a few articles of clothing and no toys, and yet they seemed joyful just being children! I remember the Navajo kids showing us how to ride a cow. Climbing onto the hump on the back was challenging, and hanging on when the cow tried to bump you off even harder, but that was their fun. They were not even allowed to listen to music, and here we were with our Walkman radios and headphones for constant entertainment. They had nothing, and yet to them, they had everything they needed.

I returned from that trip with a greater appreciation of how much I had. For a while, I felt guilty that I lived with so much. Unlike most kids, being exposed to people of color living with less happened to me quite young. Our parents made it a point to encourage me to play with kids "at the projects," as low-income housing was called back then. They didn't hesitate to take me there and help me build friendships with kids of diverse cultures and backgrounds. I was raised to remember that there is always someone with less than you; don't ever take that for granted and don't ever think that makes you better: you're only luckier.

That was my early introduction to white privilege. Now it makes sense to me that I would be drawn to work with social justice and advocating for people with needs, especially children! I am grateful to my parents and my church for introducing me to the world of social responsibility, racial equity, and inclusion.

I never want to understate the devastation of loss. Love and light alone cannot lift someone out of poverty or cure a terminal disease or bring back a loved one. But never underestimate just how powerful a difference you can make by using love and light to create a vital circle of care for those in need. It was in the caring embrace of the people of the church and the Youngs that the social worker and child advocate I would later become was born.

REFLECTION QUESTIONS

As you think about the circles of care that have made a difference in your life, ask yourself:

1. Who has been your in circles of care, and how have they offered support?
2. How have the people in your circles seen you authentically and accepted you as you are from the inside out?
3. If you were to help someone else create or discover a circle of care, where would you tell them to start?

CHAPTER 4

WHO WERE MY PARENTS?

You may be wondering about the role of my parents in developing the person I would become. As for many of you, no doubt, the legacy of my parents is complex, especially in the case of my mother. You've already met my mother twice: once as she threw me an ill-fated swimming party that inadvertently sparked my first experience with bullying, and again when her hurricane response to my injury at the local Y inadvertently gave me a glimpse of the power of light. In many ways, those two incidents reflect the inconsistency of my mother's influence: often damaging, sometimes supportive, and yet motivated with the best intentions.

My parents were of the generation influenced by the iconic characters of *Leave It to Beaver* and *The Stepford Wives*. When they first met, my father wanted his wife to be a good lawyer's spouse, available to him as needed and raising his kids while he pursued his career. My dad came home every night to a Manhattan cocktail that Mom meticulously made out of the finest whiskey, sweet vermouth, and bitters. She handed it to him while he sat in his overstuffed chair to unwind from his day.

My mother, in her June Cleaver days, a woman almost robotic in her steadfast attention to her role and routine, would fix dinner and we would all gather at the table like any good family did. What was underneath her satisfied persona, however, simmered and boiled over time into great resentment. She exhibited what I grew to understand as feminine rage. The 1970s, *Ms.* Magazine, and feminism introduced a call for women who had worked from home to leave their familiar roles and join the traditionally male workforce. Like many women of her generation, Mom was damned if she did and damned if she didn't. Women across the country had worked hard to raise families, and now they were being asked to work harder and work outside the home. Regardless of having raised her kids, been a good lawyer's wife and hosted the requisite dinner parties, and having offered herself as a volunteer, she wasn't enough. She was asked to give more.

In my teen years, my mother became increasingly agitated and depressed—a result of her marital struggles and her sense of wanting to feel like she was enough. She was easily brought to angry rants with my father, and I remember cowering in my room. She had no patience for him or me. An A– school grade would lead to recriminations of "Why didn't you get an A" and "You didn't try hard enough." Comments about how I looked or what I was wearing were endless. Every time I was made to feel inadequate, it lessened my sense of confidence, security, and wholeness. I was experiencing a series of losses that I have come to identify as *"I love you but."*

One poignant reminder of her seething anger occurred when I returned home early from a date. Exhausted from a full day, I lumbered up the steep stairs to my room and collapsed on my bed fully clothed. I was sleeping soundly when my door burst open and my mother flew to the side of my bed. She began screaming at me, accusing me of staying out past my curfew and disrespecting her rules. Before I had a chance to explain myself, she began hitting me. Uncontrollable and inconsolable, she was crying and screaming. I knew it was not really about me. It didn't take long for her to realize she was in a trance-like state, taking out all of her rising frustrations about her life on me at that moment. It was as if twenty years of growing despair and helplessness exploded. The whole incident lasted only a few minutes; then, just as quickly as she entered, she left. She froze and ran out of my room, leaving me sobbing about how much I wanted her to understand that I was trying my best to meet her expectations.

As I—now the mother of a daughter—reflect on this experience with my mother, it is clear that her anger from feeling inadequate after years of trying to meet the cultural expectations of her womanhood—being a great mother, a doting wife, an attractive woman, a kind woman, a generous woman, a lawyer's wife, an attentive daughter and daughter-in-law, a working woman in and outside the home, a role model to me, etc.—all became too much and she took it out on the one person she least wanted to hurt and most wanted to protect. It was as if she was trying to hit the pain out. I will never forget that day. It was the one and only time I was ever touched by my parents in anything other than kindness and love.

As I remember this pivotal childhood memory, I feel profound sadness for my mother's sense of her limits and inadequacies. If only she had been able to identify her loss of self and her insecurity. Maybe if she had faced her anger and attended to her feminine rage, she could have transformed it into a source of growth. She might have been able to access her feminine power and become more compassionate towards herself and others. Instead, unfortunately, she became more angry, less aware, and more depressed. She was not unlike most women of that time: confused, misunderstood, degraded, and constantly left to feel "not enough." She subconsciously passed on these issues to me, as some mothers do, and I have spent my lifetime rising up from them as well. I continue to try not to pass them on to the next generation.

And yet despite my mother's challenges, there was this surprising other side to her and (less surprisingly) to my father. I not only knew that my parents loved me, but that they also loved others. Both my mother and father instilled in me the importance of empathy for others. My mother's favorite saying came from Walter Winchell: "It's nice to be important, but it's more important to be nice."

This saying echoes in my head as I remember accompanying my parents to nursing homes to visit aging neighbors and delivering doughnuts to the Salvation Army every Tuesday night. My dad and I would sing as we drove into town, where we would stop at a small bakery and pick up their day-old doughnuts. He couldn't hold a tune, but it didn't matter. Off we would go with the words to an old Irish love song by Michael Daly, "My Wild Irish Rose," filling the car as we drove to the shelter.

I won't forget the feelings I had as a young teen handing out food to folks who were appreciative of receiving treats that we took for granted because they were a Sunday-morning staple at my house. The appreciation, the grateful expressions, and the joy-filled spirit at receiving such a simple gesture were an initiation into what my mother was trying to say by repeating Winchell's words to me. Being nice through acts of kindness and generosity was not just taught, it was lived. Whether it was my brother's hockey team visiting a nursing home or my Girl Scout troop delivering meals to shut-ins, at an early age I was immersed in a world where acts of compassion were the norm.

The other important parental influence on my life was my dad introducing us to social justice. When my father took me to the post office one day in my teens, there was a group of protesters lined up on the steps chanting their slogans about the evils of the Vietnam War. My dad, a social change agent in his own right, quietly stepped over to these people and opened the door of the post office so he could get his mail. As he made his way to the door, he silently stepped over each person crying out about the atrocities of a war they felt was unjust. I watched with awe as my father—a WWII veteran and Navy National Guard member—remained calm. I asked my dad what he had just done. He said quietly, "Katie, always remember that people have a right to protest, but I also have a right to help the people who need me as their lawyer. I needed my mail, and they needed to be heard. Hopefully, my carefully respecting their right to protest and getting my mail satisfied both of us."

My parents planted the seeds of a life of service, and they allowed me to create my sense of community. They could have prevented me from attending church and skiing with the Youngs. They could have been jealous and isolated me from my Rev, my guidance counselor Radetta, or other adult role models who supported me during this time, but instead, they embraced my need for other guidance.

I am most grateful to both my parents for that. Remembering the goodness they brought into my life is a valuable practice. Remembering the light and the love, and bringing that love to others through compassionate acts of service, were my parents' goals for my life. They recognized and supported that sensibility in me.

You will meet many parents in this book, some struggling with immense grief and hardship. And yet you will see that no matter what happened in their lives or with their children, all these parents found a way to persevere and overcome. Over time, they turned their loss into a light for others. More than anything, it is the light and the love that I remember most today about my parents.

REFLECTION QUESTIONS

As you reflect upon the people who cared for you and parented you (and these are not always biological parents)...

1. What did they value?
2. What strengths did they give you?
3. If they could impart one piece of wisdom to you today, what would they say?

CHAPTER 5

DIVERSITY AND LOSS

I have met teens who feel restless and eager to leave high school. Sometimes they are more mature than their peers, unmotivated by their classes, or want to leave early because of personal reasons. I was one of those teens. I was a music nerd who preferred serving doughnuts at the Salvation Army to going to parties. I, like many, just felt too different. Thankfully, I had a stellar guidance counselor, Radetta. When I approached her with my dissatisfaction, she didn't say what I expected; instead, she understood my desire to leave and encouraged me to consider my options.

I needed to get away and find my own sense of accomplishment and worth. I found a prep school that included high school postgraduates, so I went to night school all during my junior year to graduate at the end of my junior year and attend the prep school for one year as a post-graduate.

Some of the most well-educated and smartest people I had ever met attended this school. My roommate, Sarah, was brilliant. We had lengthy discussions about just about everything while listening to our nightly combination of the Moody Blues and Dan Fogelberg—our music reflected our differences. Sophisticated New Jersey meets down-home Vermont.

Although I had already been exposed to ethnic and social diversity thanks to my parents, my experiences here solidified inclusivity as one of my core values. There was an eclectic student body; on my floor alone were students from Harlem, Japan, Vermont, New Jersey, and China.

There, I got the chance to talk smack with my friend from Cleveland and have deep discussions about life with the daughter of a celebrity raised in Europe. When a young black woman from Mississippi got pregnant, I was her confidante as she agonized over her choice about the pregnancy. In her community, you did not pass up a chance to bring another Black life into the world. I was struck by her sense of responsibility, not only to her unborn child but to her culture and her heritage. She carried the weight of her ancestors on her back, and deciding to give birth had little to do with what she wanted and more to do with what was expected of her. She left school quickly to deal with her choice. It was hard to see her leave behind the life she had created on campus, knowing she would have to overcome many obstacles to pursue her educational dreams in the future. I knew, however, that she had the fortitude to do just that. If anyone could rise up and meet the challenge of mothering and finishing her education, it was her.

In contrast, another Black friend raised in a primarily upper-class white world was ostracized because she didn't want to engage in enough school activities related to her race. Called Oreo (black on the outside, white on the inside), her pain was palpable. She didn't fit in either of these racial worlds—another reminder that loneliness can creep in when we don't feel that our surroundings and the people we are with accept us unconditionally. In prep school, there were many reminders of the impact of race and culture and the inherent losses that occur around those factors. There, I learned that it is our responsibility to pay attention to our privileged status and take time to learn what people of color are experiencing.

This was yet another element of the social worker that was developing in me: the swirl of race, diversity, and empathy. I am so grateful to my friends from prep school who shared their honest experiences and entrusted me with their struggles to fit in as people of color.

My prep school experience and renewed sense of social responsibility led me to Lewiston, Maine, and another place where I would be led to understand so many aspects of being the best me: Bates College.

At Bates, the little light of empathy, caring, recognizing that others are worse off than you, and still finding joy would grow even brighter. Before starting my Bates experience, however, I had an encounter with a young boy who foreshadowed what would become another foundational theme of my life: the wisdom and grace of children.

REFLECTION QUESTIONS

1. What were some of the ways that you sought to belong and fit in as a young adult?
2. How did you make your choices as a young adult?
3. What were the most significant choices you made?

CHAPTER 6

◆——◆——◆

THE RESILIENCE OF A CHILD

The summer before starting college at Bates, I worked in a daycare facility where I became the swimming director. All my skills, gifts, and talents were tested on a fateful day by a spunky six-year-old who opened my mind to a new dimension of understanding loss and the complexities of how our minds support our need to remember... or in his case, to forget.

I was on lifeguard duty, looking out at a pool filled with six-year-old swimmers. With their floating devices and counselors nearby, I felt calm and reassured that all was well. I saw a young boy named Tim make his way up the steps towards the high diving board. Unusually skilled, he had passed the test to achieve this privilege that most kids could only strive toward. Startled by cries in the pool, I turned toward the commotion and whistled for some roughhousing in the shallow end to cease. Out of the corner of my eye, I could see Tim recklessly swinging on the bars atop the board. Before I had a chance to stop him, he fell. I watched with horror as his young body hit the cement floor. Gathering every ounce of speed and agility I had, I leaped to his side and, finding him unconscious, flew as fast as I could to phone 911. The ambulance came within minutes; we were part of a university campus that included a hospital. They took him away as all of us tearfully and silently prayed he would be all right. The terror I felt at the possibility of a young life under my supervision being tragically altered was beyond what I could bear. The next 24 hours limped by as I waited for news of his condition.

Thankfully, I finally received a phone call saying that remarkably, he would make a full recovery. I was stunned. Overwhelmed by the what-ifs that could have happened, I recalled the warning messages my parents had given me. They reminded me that taking responsibility for a child means not just acting in the moment, but getting the sleep and rest necessary for me as a lifeguard to remain alert, taking time to know the children and their personalities to identify who might be the risk-takers, etc. My lawyer father reminded me that when we supervise children, how we take care of ourselves matters. That one little six-year-old prepared me for many kids to come. He also left his own life lesson. After he came out of the hospital, he remarked "Katie, remember when I fell off the diving board and into the hospital?"

He had an attitude of *Oh well... next...*

Kids are so much better at that than we as adults are. We dwell on the fearful possibilities while they bounce back into the now. "When can I go back up to the high board again?" became his focus. Taking my cues from this little guy, I realized that when accidents occur, we first learn from them, and then we let them go and start making our way back up to the high diving board again and jump off into another experience.

This experience was the beginning of my desire to better understand the wisdom of children. They seem to address experiences with a better focus on what is happening immediately than we adults, who focus on the what-if's that cause us trepidation and worry. All this little guy knew was that he was okay, and it was time to lift himself back up onto the board.

Very shortly after being released from the hospital, he jumped off the high dive correctly supervised, and his smile lit up the entire pool! He believed he could, and he did!

REFLECTION QUESTIONS

Reflect on the times you have taken a risk and metaphorically jumped off the high diving board.

1. What gave you the courage to take a leap of faith?
2. Who encouraged you and who discouraged you?
3. What did you learn from the experience?

CHAPTER 7

BREAKTHROUGH AT BATES

Why did I pick a small school in Lewiston, Maine?

My college admissions effort was influenced by wanting to get away from Vermont, and two of my closest friends loved going to school in Maine. Then I narrowed it to where I felt I would fit in. When I walked into the Campus Student Center at Bates, I noticed posters on the walls addressing social issues by various social justice groups: a Gay/Straight Alliance, a peace and justice group, a racial sensitivity group—and the icing on the cake was that they were located right outside the chaplain's office. And there was a line of students gathered there! I had learned from a very young age not to miss these kinds of signs—indications that some decision was going to be in my best interest. The part of me who had discovered faith put into action in high school was drawn to those posters like a bee to honey.

I was learning and relearning that social sensitivity and an appreciation for my role in bringing that light, the feeling of connection, the voice, the nudge, and the urge to belong was very real. My life coach taught me years later that if you felt something from your head to your toes, it was an absolute "yes." Marveling at the energy around social justice outside the chaplain's office was for me the absolute "yes" for Bates!

Like every college freshman, I arrived on move-in day wide-eyed and enthusiastic about the years ahead of me. However, that old nagging people pleaser was still wreaking havoc in my psyche. I was still trying to be "enough" and looking to others to define my self-worth. When we leave home, unfortunately, we bring the voices of home with us, and I was still reeling from the blows dealt to my confidence. It didn't help when I showed up with a U-Haul trailer only to find that I was in a one-room triple. Three women and all our belongings in one room, and I had brought enough to fill it myself!

I may have felt overwhelmed and wholly inadequate, but my father left me that day with words I tried to hold on to. My parents had kissed me goodbye and walked away, and I had begun decorating our room and chatting with my new roomies when my father reappeared. He had tears in his eyes as he said, "I came to give you advice, but you don't need any advice," then he left. My dad had always been my cheerleader, and despite the ways my mother tended to break me down, he built me up, and this was no exception. Tears flowed for quite a while after that encounter. In many ways, those felt like words I had longed to hear for so long but never did, or at least they didn't sink in. His words meant that I *was* enough, that I could do this, and that all this time growing up believing and focusing on my flaws had undermined my potential. At that moment, my dad said what I needed to hear. Of course, it felt like a drop in the bucket compared to what I had needed for years.

My early months in college were seriously influenced by childhood "*I love you but*" messages and my sense of feeling less-than—a sensibility I carried forward not just from home but also from prep school. Although my grades had been good enough, they paled in comparison to the other students I came to know there. Barely 18 years old, I had spent one year in prep school with an advanced group of academically oriented students. Here, many students had been raised in private and prep schools for years, had exceptional educational records, and had accelerated their coursework through advanced exams. Not me. I struggled for every grade, and by the time I got to Bates, I was emotionally exhausted.

I began to skip classes. Unaware of what I was doing, I would sit on my bed and stare out the window at the other students passing by, making their way to the various buildings, meeting up with friends along the way. I couldn't concentrate and became despondent as I fell further and further behind. Seeking guidance and support, I spoke to a trusted adult, a psychology professor who said, "I don't think you are college material. Maybe you should make another choice." That was one of those moments when an authority figure had an opportunity to lift up a young adult and instead, in a pivotal moment when he could have been supportive, this person tore me down.

After that encounter, I gave up. I stopped going to classes and fell into a serious depression. Thankfully, I realized I needed help and went to the dean to ask for a leave of absence. Unlike the professor I spoke with, the dean recognized that time away might give me the boost I needed to come back ready to learn. After these two encounters, I chose to believe the dean. He lifted me up, gave me hope, and encouraged me. His was the message that carried the light, and with that empowerment, I decided to leave.

SPIRITUAL MUSCLES

Now what?

I called home, and my mother failed just as badly as the psychology professor, saying, "You can't drop out, you will never go back." Her vote of confidence in me was underwhelming. My father, on the other hand, did what he had always done, immediately springing into action to offer support. He showed up at my dorm five hours later, a little after midnight. We sat on the edge of my single bed, and he listened while I described my lack of motivation, my moods, and my need for a break. He took a moment and then carefully said, "I don't know that you are doing the right thing, but I will support you regardless"—stellar parental words that were just what I needed to hear. He went on to offer more golden points, stipulating that I needed to find a place to live, pay my bills, and continue taking classes at the local university so I could return to Bates the following year. I readily agreed, and the next morning, we drove the long way back through the Green Mountains.

Living on my own, paying rent, waitressing, and taking physics at the University of Vermont was the best thing I could have done. I was mastering new skills every day and learning to rely on myself, chipping away at the "I am not enough" messages that were still stuck in my head.

Wanting to support me, my mother found a Christian psychotherapist in Boston and drove me there once a month to make sure I got the best care. She knew that church and Christianity had been a fundamental aspect of my high school identity, so she thought it would help me to find someone trained in that specific modality. My mother may not have been adept at building her children up, but she certainly was proficient at finding the best coaches, equipment, schools, and the best everything. Her ambitious standards for our achievement were commensurate with her expectations of the resources we needed to accomplish anything. I have great appreciation for my mother's efforts in finding a Christian psychologist and undertaking a two-hour drive to Boston every week for six months to get me that kind of support.

He was a pastoral psychologist, someone who studied multiple religions and understood how people's beliefs impact and influence their behaviors. He, too, became one of my influencers, because as I better understood my faith and beliefs, I began to understand that faith could be like the rudder in a sailboat, helping to steer me in the best direction to achieve my goals. That light I had seen in the faces of those adults who had been supportive showed in his face, and I started to associate having a belief in something beyond oneself as the source of that light. My faith became a guiding force, an anchor, and a stabilizing force in my life. I started to see that my ability to be loved and loveable wasn't earned but instead was part of being human. Releasing the burden of proving myself freed me up to achieve my goals. I became untethered from other people's expectations and decided to develop my standards. I excelled as a waitress, got a B in physics, and paid my bills like an adult. That growth and confidence meant I was ready to return to Bates.

And I did.

Little did I know how much I would discover at Bates about the person I could become, the influences and influencers who would guide my life, and the purpose that still drives me today.

THE BIG WHY

What I had learned early on—that negative attention was better than no attention and that negative attention was a sign of caring—took a long time to stop showing up in my life. Whether I was bullied or in relationships with men who set me straight about their needs coming first,

I responded by trying to be the people pleaser. That lasted until I realized that I was attracted to these kinds of situations because my low self-esteem meant that on a subconscious level, I thought I deserved them. Having a mother who told me boys wouldn't like me if I was fat, magazines that told me I was fat even though I could see in the photos of myself I wasn't, and a faith message that taught me to always be kind meant I was set up to be put down and taken advantage of for a good part of my life. I obliged by repeatedly putting myself in situations where I victimized myself over and over and then got angry that it happened.

The layers of loss in my life were revealing more to me about who I had been, how I had been treated, and who I wanted to become. I was ready to lift myself up to a wiser, stronger version of myself. Each of those situations represented another loss, moving further away from the authentic me who had existed when I was born. Mirroring the goodness and light that I attracted made the difference in how I navigated through those losses. Bates was the beginning of my understanding of this.

One of my greatest teachers, Professor Tom Tracy, taught classes about how individuals were inspired with passion and purpose, and that their differing faith experiences led them onward. Tom's classes became a beacon for me. I felt led by the wisdom I was hearing as I studied these great thinkers and changemakers. Tom had a way of instructing his students to think about themselves, what was motivating them, and how to dig deep and discover who they were meant to be. To this day, I still use information from those classes in my work. I even touched base with Tom about a client's story just recently. He is retired now, and we may not be in touch, but his presence in my life is very much like a lighthouse to which I turn when I need it.

It wasn't until Tom's classes at Bates, where I began studying heroes, heroines, and people whose faith had given them strength and courage, that I started to realize I had choices. Studying Malcolm X, Harriet Tubman, Joan of Arc, and other religious changemakers ignited a fire in me. The light inside was becoming a flame, a fierce determination to learn as much as I could about humanity and why people do what they do so that I could help them reach their potential.

Bates is where I found so many influencers who reminded me that I could transform my passion for service and helping others into a lifetime commitment to being a compassionate change-maker.

Of course, there was also that other part of going to college. One day, I walked into class with a headache raging, my mouth dry as a desert, and my thinking about as clear as mud, but I was there. Attending a Philosophy of Religion course when you are hungover from a trip to the local watering hole nicknamed The Goose leaves one vulnerable.

My professor asked me a question: "Katie, what would you say if you were a nun during the Reformation?" In normal circumstances, I would recall some passage from the reading that would illustrate his point that a nun would be torn in her beliefs as the roles of women were changing, but the only words I could muster were, "I could never be a nun!" Of course, the class roared, and even the professor chuckled and realized he had better move on to someone else. Drinking in college was part of learning how to be responsible and when to make sure you have your faculties in class. I learned that lesson from this situation because as you can imagine, I didn't stop being teased about it for quite a while.

Other than learning to navigate drinking, college was an awakening to a way of thinking about people. In my religion and history courses, I began to develop a sense of asking what influences people's choices on a macro and micro level. The Reformation example is just one of many times I was taught to delve deeply into the psychological, emotional, cultural, social, and spiritual influences on a human's choices. Geoff Law, my history teacher, didn't just teach historical facts; he challenged us to think as if we were living in the period we were studying.

It was no longer enough for me to ask questions about how I made decisions; many events challenged me to dig down and take a deep dive into who I was and my *why* as it related to the direction of my life.

When a classmate's mother suddenly died, I was thrown into a situation where death was something I desperately needed to know more about. Trying to comfort someone with sudden grief was new to me, and I, being the good college student that I was, needed to know as much as I could about how to support him. It was then that I discovered a book by a woman who would be a lifelong mentor and friend. This Swiss physician and change agent in the field of death and dying became one of the most vital influencers in my life. Her little book, *On Death and Dying*, became equal to my Bible in importance as a guiding force. The concept of listening to the dying was something that resonated with me. Listening became a central theme in my life, and my relationship with Elisabeth Kübler-Ross began.

THE MESSAGE

One sunny autumn day, I looked out at people wearing the uniform of a small New England college: the preppy look of L.L. Bean Shetland sweaters and chinchilla draped over shoulders, various styles of jeans, and the signature shoes—loafers or sneakers with no socks. A sea of Lily Pulitzer wearing hot pink and aqua stood nearby: I could hear them giggling and gossiping about the keg party from the night before. It was rush hour, with students intersecting and emerging from all different directions from the antique brick buildings that made up the Bates quad. The stone chapel with its regal presence stood in the background as a constant reminder of the faith-based roots of this now fully secular institution. The founder, a social advocate from the 1800s who insisted that anyone, regardless of gender, race, religious beliefs, etc., could be admitted, made our school the first college in New England to go co-ed. Freedom and civil rights were foundational principles emanating from classes throughout our college.

I walked past the crowds congregated in small groups on the velvety green grass underneath the cascading oak trees and headed to my favorite spot: an iron bench a few steps from where the Hawthorne building, standing stately with its white pillars and steep stone steps and bell tower, marked the center of campus. This was where I took all my religion courses, contemplated life, death, evil, and hope, and studied the lives of social leaders like Malcolm X and Martin Luther King.

It was a bit cold, but facing the sun I felt the warmth on my face as I sat down to ponder the lessons of my class on evil. The writings of Kierkegaard, Bonhoeffer, and Nietzsche swirled in my mind. Existential questions about my own beliefs—and an unsettling realization that I wasn't sure what they really were—left me with a deep sense of isolation. Once certain of my Christian ideas, I was now being challenged to think differently, to critique what was once taught as truth, and this left me feeling separate and apart from the crowd of people right in front of me. Their collective voices were a distant background noise as they bustled past each other to get to their next class. Despite the bell sounding behind me, I was caught up in my thoughts and sat silently wondering about my future, why was I here, where was I going to go—all the questions a conscientious junior in college mutters to themselves on a sunny day in May.

Then I felt a calm, quiet sense of presence come over me, and a thought entered my mind as if it was being placed there: "You will create children's hospice programs in many places." Startled by the clarity of the message, I sat there for quite a while, wondering about this statement and where it came from. Was this a thought? A call? A message from somewhere beyond me? Tingling from my head to my toes, I chose to believe the voice that spoke to me. I decided to pursue more information, starting with, "What is *hospice*?"

REFLECTION QUESTIONS

1. What challenged you during your transition into adulthood?
2. Did you struggle with confidence?
3. Who were the adults who lifted you up?

CHAPTER 8

DR. ELISABETH KÜBLER-ROSS AND THE CALLING

After this experience of being "called," I became obsessed with learning everything I could about death, dying, and grief. The only book I could find to help guide me was Elisabeth Kübler-Ross' seminal work, *On Death and Dying*. Elisabeth's stories offered wisdom that unlocked a direction that had been with me since I was a child, which was to listen for some message that was beyond me but within me. Elisabeth believed that if we paid attention, we would hear, recognize, or somehow understand that our most significant role as humans is to live as if we were dying. Her dying patients taught her how to live, as one of my favorite quotes from her work explains.

> "It is not the end of the physical body that should worry us. Rather, our concern must be to live while we're alive— to release our inner selves from the spiritual death that comes with living behind a facade designed to conform to external definitions of who and what we are." (*Death: The Final Stage of Growth*, 1975).

In other words, every loss is an opportunity to learn more about life.

From reading Kübler-Ross and learning more about how our beliefs drive our behavior, I started to put together a life's purpose that fit like the pieces of a puzzle with my past experiences and who I wanted to become. Maybe that voice I heard when sitting on that bench was my inner wisdom. Maybe it was my intuition. Maybe it was from somewhere beyond me. Maybe that's God? As always, I had questions, many questions, but my choice to listen to the influences of Elisabeth Kübler-Ross and the lessons from my classes in college would lead me to a path that would include children, death, and butterflies.

BUTTERFLIES

When Elisabeth Kübler-Ross visited the Majdanek Nazi concentration camp in 1946, she found what was to become a symbol associated with her work with death and dying. It also represented what I was discovering in my own life: that people find hope in their own way even amid great tragedy. On the walls of the barracks that housed children who were soon to be gassed, Elisabeth was deeply moved to see many images of butterflies drawn with stones dug into the walls. It was as if the children were drawing winged symbols of hope.

Elisabeth began to see in her dying patients what she saw in these drawings: the effect of re-birth. She authored a beautiful book depicting the power of the butterfly.

It amazes me now when I recall how intrigued I was as a child by the butterflies that I walked past on the way home from school every day. Little did I know as a child growing up in Vermont that these colorful insects of beauty and grace would become even more prevalent in my adult life. They would represent my work and understanding that in the process of facing loss, grief allows us to delve deeply into our cocoon of healing, and over time, we can emerge with a newer, stronger version of ourselves. Like the heroes I studied in college, we all possess this capability to re-discover ourselves as if we are returning to our birth and re-discovering how to live.

The rugged road I grew up on was worn with potholes from people making their way to their summer cottages on Lake Champlain in Vermont. As one of the few kids who lived there year-round, I looked forward to fall, when the crowds cleared out and I could once again take off on my bike to explore nature in solitude. Flanked on either side by pussy willows, cattails, and milkweed plants, our road offered me a choice spot for collecting cocoons to hatch into butterflies. I remember with fondness the hours I spent collecting grass to feed the caterpillar and watching with great anticipation as he ate his way into spinning his tiny home. Once the cocoon was complete, I would rush home from school and into the little kitchen in the back of our house to see if my little miracle was ready to happen. Gingerly placing milkweed into the grass, I awaited the butterfly's birth.

For me, as for so many of us, butterflies have symbolized many distinct aspects of my life. As a child, it meant the anticipation and wonder of witnessing a new life being born. As I got older, butterflies represented childhood memories of running in the tall grass of the fields across from my house.

When I went to college and began to study death and dying, the butterfly became a symbol associated with the end of life—and a belief that with death, there is rebirth. Elisabeth Kübler-Ross' story about the butterflies and dying children resonated with me. I could almost feel in my soul the experiences of those children as they neared death and yet remained hopeful. All these experiences foreshadowed the message I received that day at Bates: *You will create children's hospice programs.* I didn't know at the time how significant those two themes—children and dying—were becoming. Through the years, I would work with so many children facing incredible pain and hardship with resilience and the will to be happy. Like Jason, these children—some of whom died while others lived with life-long challenges—would become my luminaries, teaching me some of my life's most valuable lessons. You'll meet many of them in this book. I designed this logo to honor their ability to hold onto hope while anticipating death.

I was lucky enough to encounter one of these luminaries at Bates. His name was Max.

CHAPTER 9

DIVING INTO THE DARK

Combining my skill as a swimmer and experience as a lifeguard with my new interests in understanding how children find hope amid struggle, it was no surprise that I jumped at the opportunity to teach blind children how to swim.

I remember walking past empty lockers with their doors slightly ajar to reveal the Bates Bobcat sports paraphernalia every Bates College athlete owned. I could hear the laughter and the metal doors slamming as I "peacocked" my way to the Athletic Director's office. Entering the office walking confidently with my chest out and my head held high, I sat down in front of the Director's metal desk, which was covered with files, papers, and a variety of sports-related books, and handed him a list of my swimming-related experience: YWCA Camp Counselor, Director, Youth Swimming, Lifeguard. I could hear giggles and smell the familiar combination of sweaty bodies and sweet soap as steam emanated from the showers. I fidgeted in the tall wooden chair as I waited for his answer. He looked over my resume and leaned in closer to me as I waited, barely breathing, and said: "You have the job. You will be instructing school-aged kids ages eight to ten, preparing them for Special Olympics."

Teaching blind kids to swim—me, directing a new program! I was elated. I couldn't wait to share the news with anyone who would listen. *What an honor!* I thought to myself. I grabbed a power bar out of my locker, put on a warm woolen jacket, and headed to my dorm.

The next weeks passed slowly. Finally, the day arrived, and I walked into the Olympic-sized pool with the cool blue tile that enhanced its size and made it feel even greater. There they were, my protégés: six legally blind swimmers, waiting for me. *Me*, the person who was going to help them face their greatest fear: swimming in darkness. I pulled my shoulders back, leaned forward, took a deep breath, and began to teach the basics: how to hold your breath and breathe out, how to move your arms. I gently assisted them, adjusting their arms in circles to simulate the movement, until they began to catch on and repeat the crawl stroke action. Then it was time to get into the water. One by one, each child, holding the hand of a trusted adult foster family member, was led into the water.

One courageous child in particular, Max, stood out as an exceptional swimmer. I stood in awe witnessing this eight-year-old blind-from-birth marvel fiercely making his way past his fear and moving inch by inch toward the goal of participating in the Special Olympics. I witnessed his trust, despite the void in his visual capacity, that he could comprehend where it was safe for him to be. He carefully counted the steps at the edge of the pool and lowered himself in. No one held his hand and no one told him where the water's edge lay. He knew. How? He had faith in something none of us could ever comprehend: his internal guidance. So many times I held my breath as I watched him approach the pool because, of course, his steps measured differently each time. There was no way for him to calculate his movement exactly, so instead, he relied on his own sense of when he needed to stop. We stood ready if he took a misstep, but remarkably, he never did.

Over time, he became steadily more confident in relying on his strength and agility to enter what must have been for him a terrifying experience—but one that he found a way to resiliently master. Max was the first to enter the deep end; he even asked me to allow him to jump in. Positioned in the water, I caught him as he soared through the air into my arms.

Max was boisterous, with a wonderful sense of humor. He would wink at my commands and at times lean in and stare as if he was looking right through me. We spent weeks together while he learned to swim the free stroke. He learned to gracefully glide through what for him was wet and black, counting on me to call out "Stop!" when he was inches from the edge. His wide grin, the gleam in his eye, and his endless questions left me proud to be his instructor.

Watching him methodically make his way across the pool, gradually gaining the confidence to add speed, was literally witnessing "blind faith." He trusted in what he couldn't see. I began, at the tender age of 20, to grasp what it meant to truly take a leap of faith: to jump into a situation without the ability to know the outcome, trusting that somehow, I would always be ok.

My faith in Max left me vulnerable to criticism from others. "I am not sure this is good for him," said Shirley, an adult who often used the pool after our class. With her severe grey Dorothy Hamill haircut and black polka-dotted skirted bathing suit, she was a tall, formidable presence. "You are getting this kid's hopes up that he will be able to compete for the Special Olympics. He's blind—that's just not realistic!"

I felt my jaw clench and my eyes narrow as I listened to her concern. "He is making great progress," I found myself saying. "He would be crushed if we slowed down." With my back straight and my posture rigid, I walked around her towards the locker room.

"Don't forget to lock the door," I heard her edgy, piercing voice call out. She was worried that the kids would find their way back to the pool from the locker room and hurt themselves or end up in the water unintentionally. To prevent that, I locked the door once all the kids were in the locker room after their lesson. "Of course!" I hollered back. "Of course, I will!"

Max continued to progress, and he and the other kids now wanted us to teach them how to measure their steps and walk back and forth from the pool to the locker room without assistance. At the Special Olympics, they would be asked to do this with a supportive adult next to them. *"Please,"* they begged, "We know we can. We want to do it ourselves."

"Well, we can try it. Who can walk out the steps with me?" They all measured their steps carefully as the adults cheered them on.

The children, once only capable of small, hesitant movements, were now walking with deliberate, strong steps and easing themselves in and out of the pool, laughing and cheering each other on. Swimming without physical assistance, they swam from one end to the other, trusting themselves and the adults who were swimming beside them. The adults, pleased with the progress of all the children, stopped to hug and thank me profusely for giving these children an opportunity they thought they would never have. To see them swim—to see them find within themselves the courage to discover trust matched only by the depth of the pool—filled me with a sense of awe.

One day, Max was particularly giddy. He had shortened his time to swim two lengths of the lane by five seconds. When it was time to leave, he pleaded for a chance to stay a bit longer. "Please, Miss Katie, can't we just do a little more?" he asked. "I know I can get even better."

"I am sorry, Max," I told him, "We have to go."

For some reason, that day the pool was unusually cold, and my legs and arms had developed goosebumps, so I was eager to get out. Watching as each child filed out of the pool toward the locker room, I was shivering and wanted my towel. Turning my back for just a few seconds, I rushed into the locker room for it. Although it felt like seconds, it was just long enough for Max to walk back into the pool room. I froze as I returned to see him standing close to the edge. I called out, "Max, what are you doing in here?"

"I told you I could do even better if we had just a little more time," he said. I grabbed his shoulders and whisked him into the locker room, then stopped to close and lock the doors. I found myself hoping no one had seen me break the cardinal rule of lifeguarding: taking your eyes off the swimmers. But no—of course there was Shirley, making sweeping arm gestures at me and screeching, "How could you? How could you put these poor children at risk?!"

I slunk back into the locker room, my stomach tied in a knot, and helped the children finish getting ready to leave. When they were all gone, I collapsed onto the wooden bench by my locker and wept.

The director's office, which was once my place of triumph, was now the opposite. I tried to angle myself away from the face staring at me and saying the words I had been dreading: "You are fired, and the program will end effective immediately." I barely heard the explanation of the athletic director as he repeated, "We have to end the program." The words felt like daggers plunged deep into my heart, sending a flood of tears to my eyes that stung almost as much as the words.

"I am so, so sorry," was all I could say.

I could see that he felt burdened by having to say this, but after gently placing his hand on my shoulder as if to say he too was sorry, he left me there alone. I knew it hadn't been easy for him or anyone else, but one of the first rules of safety when lifeguarding minors is to lock the locker room door so no one can get back into the pool unsupervised. Of *course* I knew this. Holding my breath, I sighed and thought, *"Why didn't I heed Shirley's warning?"*

I don't know if Max made it to the Special Olympics that year because I wasn't allowed to have any contact with him, but for me, he will always be a special champion. All the swimmers, but he most of all, taught me that there is a voice inside that will quietly alert us to danger if we listen to it. But if we don't pay attention, there can be dire consequences.

This deep loss led me right back to all my insecurities, to the voices of "less than" and "incapable" and "of course you screwed up." Dejected, forlorn, and feeling overwhelmed with the sense of having let down so many people, I carried that grief into my next choice point.

I decided that despite how I felt about myself, instead of removing myself from service as a failure, I would learn from this experience and become more mature, wiser, and more attentive. Instead of dismissing my challenges, I would be more aware of them, which would help me understand them better. Again, reflecting on the lives and choices of the heroes and heroines of my religion classes, I decided to channel my own Joan of Arc determination and rise from this experience determined to serve with more patience and less self-focus.

In one of my first ventures into supporting children, this was a particularly challenging loss that required time, space, and good therapy for me to come back and try again. A harsh lesson. One that I have not ever forgotten.

REFLECTION QUESTIONS

Reflect on a moment when an inner voice told you to make a certain choice.

1. Did you listen?
2. If yes, what was the outcome?
3. If not, why not?

CHAPTER 10

TROUBLED TEENS: NEW LESSONS IN CIRCLES OF CARE

Despite the disastrous end to my work with the blind swimmers, I would not be deterred and continued to seek out opportunities for volunteer service while still at Bates. This quest led me to a group of teenagers in what we then called a halfway house. It referred to a place where someone who was struggling with drugs or alcohol—or in this case, behavioral issues—went to receive intensified treatment before moving to their next home.

I walked into a large living room with bookshelves flanking the plain, cream-colored walls and saw a group of teens ranging from twelve to eighteen years old sitting in a circle. They were clad in t-shirts and jeans and had forlorn looks on their faces, letting me know right away that I was one of many who had come and gone, and they had no interest in anything I had to say. Struggling with their lack of comments or responses, my first instinct was to run away—to leave them behind, to go back to my sheltered little world in my dorm and my three meals a day and my L.L.-Bean-Shetland-sweater existence. What did I have to teach them? Still reeling from my recent firing, those negative voices were loud in my thoughts. As the blank stares bore into my soul and revealed every insecurity, I was perplexed, overwhelmed, and feeling completely inadequate... until I combined my lessons from Max and Elisabeth. Then I realized I needed to meet them in their world, to ask *them* to tell *me* what hadn't worked for them and how they had been let down by other people who had tried to help them.

One of the many lessons I learned from Max was to dive into the dark—make yourself vulnerable and trust that there will be a way for you to move forward. At that moment, I was like Max, searching for a way to make it through what I could not fully understand: how these youth felt about life and what they needed. I resolved to walk to the edge and ask them to teach me! How could I be different? What could they teach me about what they needed?

One thing is certain: teenagers are not used to being asked these kinds of questions. These kids especially. Bounced from residential facilities to foster homes and group homes, they had little to say and little control over their lives. Asking them what they would like from me was new.

At first, thrown by the question, they were silent, but I could see in their eyes that they were contemplating an answer. One by one, stories poured out about their lack of choices in every area of their lives. They had felt silenced, unnoticed, unheard, overlooked. The descriptions of feeling lost and abandoned poured out of them like lava from an overflowing volcano. Once I found the opening, each week there was more sharing and more disturbing stories of rape, incest, physical abuse, and neglect—so much pain and suffering for such young people.

But I listened to each story of horrendous loss and suffering. And remembering that insight from Elisabeth Kübler-Ross about the importance of lessons from loss, I began to see that by bearing witness to their stories, I validated their emotions, their reactions, and their experiences; I validated *them*. I thought of the words of Kübler-Ross about listening to the dying and how their stories taught her how to live, and I recognized the same dynamic in my experience with these youth. It was the value that feeling heard had on their effort to heal.

When I was a teenager, I had found in Karen, her family, and her church a circle of care that I never experienced before. They were willing to listen to me, respect me, and tell me that I was worthwhile. In my own way, I was offering what the Youngs and church had offered me to these troubled teenagers: a first opportunity to be heard.

Years later, my volunteer work at the halfway house influenced my work as a therapist with teenagers Rick and Sam.

RICK AND SAM

Sometimes, children are not privileged to live with a "Leave It to Beaver" family or in a neighborhood that provides the sense of caring we all crave. Rick had no family or place to live, but he had drive—a passion for living and a motivation unlike anyone I have ever known.

I remember the day he walked into my office. This 14-year-old strutted in like he owned the place. He sat down and proceeded to tell me he needed help because he was living on the streets, and he really wanted to stay safe and find a way out of his struggles. As he plopped into a chair, his arms folded in his lap, I didn't pay attention to his haggard face or well-worn clothes or tousled hair. What caught my eye was the sadness and determination in his deep brown eyes. His story was one of true resilience. Not only did he keep coming to therapy, but he also attended night school and public high school while living in shelters and managing to find odd jobs to pay for what he needed. He did not miss a session, and his dedication to understanding his traumatic past was fueled by a sense of wanting to take his story and help others.

An opportunity arose one day right in my office. I had a hunch that what might help him feel valuable—which is what he longed for—was to help another of my clients. Thankfully, when I approached my supervisor, she readily agreed that pairing two struggling teens, the other living in a foster home, might benefit both. Little did I know at the time that this was to become a theme in my work. Giving Rick and Sam a sense of purpose helped each feel valued, which in turn gave them even more resolve to continue their healing process. Sharing their individual layers of loss brought them comfort as they mirrored the kindness and acceptance they lacked being on their own without family for each other. In my office, they pulled together and helped each other survive. As they built each other up, their mutual encouragement created a bond that helped them overcome the haunting memories of abuse and the negative self-statements that had been with them since birth.

Their friendship and my witnessing of their healing was one of my earliest experiences with creating a circle of care. I bore witness to the healing that happens when life's challenges are seen and validated. I also learned the power of peer support when adults get out of the way of the wisdom of a teenager. Sometimes they know more than adults do about what they need. I was blessed by these two boys because they illuminated that resilience becomes magnified when it is seen by another.

Rick went on to college, and last I heard, he had found a profession that allowed him to serve others. I am not sure what happened to Sam, but I do not doubt that he, too, rose and became whoever he envisioned. Rick and Sam epitomized the resilient capacity in all of us. They truly lit a fiery spirit in each other and in all of us who knew them.

REFLECTION QUESTIONS

Reflect upon who among your peers has lifted you up.

1. How are your needs met in your peer relationships?
2. How difficult is it for you to ask your peers for help?
3. What one thing would you share with your peers that you learned about yourself?

CHAPTER 11

THE CHILD WITHIN

I had always been the little kid who looked up with wonder and listened, who saw the mist on the water or the moss on the tree, or who heard the slightest variation of tones in a piece of music. I look and listen for the magic. It's usually subtle, but for some reason, I have been gifted with the ability to see the ripple in the air when the whale spouts or hear the fifth level of harmony in *The Messiah*. This has meant learning to look and listen for "the signs." When Green Mountain Katie climbed mountains, took off on long bike rides to contemplate life, or took long walks channeling her inner Anne of Green Gables, she was developing an appreciation and understanding of silence and the value of stillness. I learned the value of taking a pause and carefully considering my next words. My intuition and creative internal messenger could send me creative and valuable ideas. As a young social worker in my first job after college, I found some innovative ways to support my clients.

§

After college, I began working with the severely mentally ill at a counseling center run by three amazing middle-aged women. At 24 years young, I was a challenge to them. Still thinking I had the world by the tail with all my college knowledge, I was arrogant and unprepared for the population of folks who were my new responsibility. These wonderful souls were in and out of hospitals and suffered hallucinations, delusions, and paranoia. Heavily medicated, they were docile most of the time and very much like dependent children. A snotty wise-ass twenty-something faced a big hurdle trying to connect with these quiet individuals. Their world was simple and contained. They did arts and crafts and cared for one another. Our role was to help them make good social choices and to support them in feeling good about themselves while helping them understand their limitations when they needed help. In my youth and inexperience, I thought I had nothing to offer and little to learn, but was I ever wrong!

MARIE

In the 1980s, we were given opportunities to leave the office with our clients. It was understood that mentally ill folks were more comfortable in their own homes. I had this one client, Marie, whom I met at the beach near her home for therapy. She lived in a very tiny apartment, and we both enjoyed the space and freedom the beach offered us. She loved to walk in and out of the waves. Raised in France, she was an 80-year-old woman who spoke very quietly with a thick French accent. She dressed in simple frocks, and as a woman of very few words, it was challenging for me to be able to help her. One day, when the waves were reaching her knees, I noticed a spark in her eyes, a glimmer of energy and enthusiasm. Somehow this older, quiet woman was a young girl playing in the waves. She was a child again. Drawing from my experiences with children swimming, I decided to take a risk and join her. The two of us were splashing in the water, and Marie started to share stories about her family and how she had felt free in the water growing up. She described a recurring dream she had of swimming toward her family, who were sitting in front of the hearth by a warm fire, but every time she got close to them, a large wave would push her backward. Intrigued by her love of the waves and her dream message that waves would push her away, I had an idea: What if she could allow a wave to rush over her? Would the metaphor of not being pushed away from her family offer her any comfort?

The next time we met, she wore her bathing suit, and we stood in the waves together. As I described her dream, I asked her what would happen if she found herself going underneath the wave. Would it allow her to get closer to her family? She lit up like a light and started to repeat the word

DUCK! Then like magic, I watched this sweet, quiet woman become five years old, ducking with delight as each wave rushed over her. Gleefully she kept ducking and chanting her new mantra. From then on, we were able to talk about her fear of getting close to her family because she was afraid of being hurt—a fear mitigated by her newfound power to *duck* and allow their insults or hurtful comments to wash over her. Her depression was reduced, and she became much more animated. It was a sad day when wave therapy had to end for budgetary reasons, but I never forgot the power of that childlike innocence releasing our minds from the *shoulds* of how adults are supposed to behave. In this, my first job as an adult mental health provider, understanding the power of treating the child within became an important asset that contributed to my growth as a listening, creative, supportive therapist.

REFLECTION QUESTIONS

Reflect on the child within.

1. How at ease are you with being spontaneous and childlike?
2. What losses do you relate to your family of origin?
3. What losses would you most like to heal from your family relationships?

CHAPTER 12

THE RASPBERRY: MEETING DR. ELISABETH KÜBLER-ROSS

Roberta, one of the three women who ran the counseling center where I met Marie, is my mentor to this day. She was instrumental in helping me further understand the work of Elisabeth Kübler-Ross, who taught that underlying any painful experience, there is always loss. If we delve into our experience of loss, we discover who and what we value about living. It was no coincidence that it was Roberta who introduced me to another mentor.

Roberta had invited me to attend an Elisabeth Kübler-Ross workshop. We drove down a dirt road and saw farm animals grazing and then got a peek at the apple orchards. It was quintessential Maine: a retreat center with simplistic farm-like architecture, big porches with rocking chairs, and a large conference room where we would all meet and share our losses. At twenty-four years old, I barely had enough years behind me to recognize any significant issues. But I was following the call I received at Bates to pursue death, dying, and grief work—and who better to learn from than the death and dying guru herself?

One by one, people came to the front where Elisabeth was seated. Beside her were notes and gifts that her many admirers hoped she would notice. There was one particular gift, a vase that Elisabeth didn't notice amid the coffee and chocolate stash that had been strategically placed in her hands' reach. As she was speaking, Elisabeth reached down, thinking she was collecting her favorite German chocolate, and instead pulled up a handful of ashes. Then we heard a loud, "Oh no, she picked up George!" Recognizing that someone had placed their loved one at her feet, she recovered quite well, and we all shared a hearty belly laugh! Then, with the sacred attention due to such occasions, we gave reverence to George as his recent widow described her grief.

This workshop was the beginning of many experiences that taught me the value of life lessons from loss. Each person shared gut-wrenching experiences of either their impending death or that of someone who had passed. Tears, anger, frustration, excruciating pain—all were exhibited by those who dared to sit in front of Elisabeth and share their hurt.

I have no idea what drew me to the front that day, but it resulted in the beginning of a many-year friendship and mentorship that lasted until Elisabeth's death. I remember sheepishly kneeling on the mat and lifting the bat that people had been using to beat out all their raging emotions. I started to hit a pillow very softly, muttering a few words about how my parents hadn't offered me self-confidence, trying desperately to find an appropriate source of grief. Alas, I was too young and didn't know myself well enough to authentically grieve in front of 100 strangers. Elisabeth, sensing my discomfort, tried to draw me out with questions, but in my twenty-four-year-old lack of insight, I basically went silent. Then I made the huge mistake of saying, "I really don't have any losses"—to which Elisabeth stuck her tongue out, blew a raspberry, and uttered her famous reprimand: "Phony baloney!"

I could have been humiliated, crushed, or embarrassed, but instead, I chose to be intrigued and to wonder, "Why did that just happen?" Later that day, walking down the hall, I came face-to-face with Elisabeth, and without any prompting, we both kissed our fingers and raised them to the heavens, and she smiled. This was one of the times I knew I had received a sign. I had no idea at the time what a profound influence she would have on my life, but our intuitive, spontaneous gesture meant something, and I knew it.

When I met her again 20 years later, this moment came back to me. We were in sync, and there was a reason I was to meet her again, become a follower, build a relationship with her foundation, and become a consultant for social change teaching her theories. So many magical moments have occurred in my life that can't be explained rationally. Meeting this amazing

Swiss powerhouse was one of those moments. Her presence in my life is why I chose to use the word INSPIRITED to identify her influence on me. The spirit of her teaching is the foundation for all that I do.

REFLECTION QUESTIONS

1. Have you ever met someone, and you just knew the encounter happened for a reason?
2. Were you open to the message that explained—immediately or perhaps much later—the reason you met?
3. How did your life change as a result?

CHAPTER 13

"THE HELPERS ARE HERE!"

Sometime after meeting Dr. Kübler-Ross for the first time, I became unhappy and unsettled—that familiar feeling that told me change was afoot, but I hadn't quite figured out what it was or how I would make it happen. The work I had done with patients like Marie and others had grounded me in the principles of grief, and my experience with Elisabeth at the retreat had given me a framework for learning how to live and grow with loss. It was time for me to move closer to working with death and dying.

Roberta wasn't at all surprised that I was ready to move. She had helped me grow to a place where a voice was calling me to follow a bigger dream. When I spoke to her about my spiritual quest, Roberta was thrilled and sent me off to Boston University School of Theology with all her good wishes and blessings. Why BU? Because they had a combined field of study in theology and social work, and most importantly, I was following in the footsteps of one of my heroes: Martin Luther King.

At BU, Professor Merle Jordan, a nationally recognized professor of pastoral psychology, brilliantly helped me and others find the voice to unconditionally encourage and empower people of any belief or faith tradition to work through loss.

My seminary experience was rich with daily enlightening moments. There was a time when Palestinian and Israeli students came together to talk about their conflicts, and we were privileged as members of the seminary to join the discussion. Their message to us as white observers was clear: "Do not be white rescuers! Let *us* define our battles. Only *we* know what we truly need. You can enter our discussion as an observer, but you cannot understand because you will not go through what we have endured."

It was a lesson I will never forget. People of distinct cultures, especially when they are engaged in conflicts, are the only ones who have the privilege to identify what that conflict is and is not. The "rescuing whites," as we were described, can never understand their needs; only *they* can articulate them.

So many times throughout my career I have drawn from the teachings of Merle Jordan and my training at BU. Thanks to Merle, later in my career this Christian woman was able to provide comfort to a Muslim family losing a child and to an Arab sheik whose two wives were trying to manage his hospice care. Those are just two of many examples of how I held the value of this lesson in supporting people from diverse backgrounds.

My experience of understanding different beliefs was further challenged by my introduction to feminist theology and thought. I had never heard anyone question the depiction of a God figure as anything but male. The Anna Howard Shaw Center, named after the first female ordained minister, who was also a physician, was a resource center at the BU School of Theology. It offered access to articles by the Stone Center, a center of feminist knowledge located at Wellesley College, that provided resources challenging us to expand our view of ourselves as Christian women.

Throughout my life, I have learned from so many different people in vastly different circumstances. And no doubt, so have you. Perhaps not a ground-breaking pioneer in your field of work, or a dying high school football hero who fought to leave a legacy of love, or a wise theologian who taught his students that while faiths are different, pain is universal; my teachers are different from yours because we find the teachers we *need*.

Unfortunately, sometimes we may not see our teachers. We may not realize that they are near us and ready to offer lessons that can help us accept and grow through our challenging experiences. To recognize our teachers and their lessons, we must be aware of our needs and alert to their presence in our lives. During early sessions with my clients, I ask them to become *awake, aware,* and *alert.* I urge them to take quiet time in stillness or to move with a quiet mind so they can pay attention to the people and experiences that come into their lives—people and experiences that can help them overcome their loss.

Anyone who has offered us guidance and support, shared their wisdom and insight, and brought light into our darkness is our teacher. And when we need them, they will be there, perhaps physically or perhaps only in our minds and our hearts. As Fred Rogers said, "Look for the helpers!"

And they come to you in the most unexpected ways. As I walked along Commonwealth Avenue on the riverside urban campus of Boston University, little did I know that after Merle Jordan and the feminists I discovered at the Anna Howard Shaw Center, I would meet my next set of teachers in the most unexpected of places.

REFLECTION QUESTIONS

1. Who or what are or have been your greatest mentors or teachers?
2. What valuable lessons did they teach you?
3. Who would you be if you had never met them?

CHAPTER 14

THE REVEREND MRS.

One of my favorite sayings is, "Life is what happens while you are making other plans." It's a quote attributed to Allen Saunders that refers to what I have witnessed repeatedly in my life and the lives of others: unexpected change happens. Such was the case when I set off to seminary. I was determined to pursue my calling and make my mark on the world. I wasn't at all expecting to fall in love, get married, and move to another part of the country… yet that's what ultimately happened.

Sometimes loss happens as part of something we expect to bring us great joy. Our choices may bring us into a situation where despite our good intentions, we simply don't fit. This leaves us feeling a sense of longing for what is familiar and comforting. This was my experience after I left the seminary. Suddenly, I was thrown into situations that compromised my values and it left me feeling a great sense of loss, especially of my identity.

In my first weeks of class at BU, I met a kind, loving social justice advocate with a charming accent who swept me off my feet—so much so that we became inseparable. To quote one of my professors, I focused on "the good stuff." We shared a deep passion for the underserved, the downtrodden, the poor, the lowly—whatever language applies to those in need. Will reminded me of my father as he stood with righteous resolve for positive social change.

When Will asked me to marry him, I said yes. Naïve and optimistically feeling a sense of renewed meaning and purpose, I was ready to assume a new role.

When Will graduated, I decided to leave behind my studies, join him, and assume a new role. I felt I had learned what I needed to pursue my career, and there was an excellent university near his new job where I could continue my degree in social work. I convinced myself that we were ready, and we set out for a new life together. Unfortunately, I had no idea how demanding the life of a youth pastor would be—or that his wife would also have duties and responsibilities.

I cannot say enough about the love and kindness of the people in the community where we served. It was a small, close-knit community—so much so that when I moved into town, the local sheriff pulled me over when he saw that I had out-of-town plates to see who I was!

Everyone tried hard to welcome me, but the New Englander in me had a tough time accepting the racial disparity of where I lived. One of my first evenings as a minister's wife, a sixteen-year-old girl came to our door after having a belt taken to her for going to the movies with a Black boy. Stunned and alarmed about the acceptance of what felt completely unacceptable to me, a loneliness and a sense of social isolation began in the disparity between the behavior of the community and my perceptions of racism and sexism.

BATTLING RACISM

As a white woman living in what felt like a segregated community, I came to understand that my sense of loss became an opportunity for personal growth. How could I unconditionally accept a group of people and a place where people thought so differently than I did?

I decided to continue my studies and the pursuit of my calling by getting a master's degree in social work from a nearby university. But perhaps the greatest learning came from my experiences with the good people of this new community that I grew to love.

As part of my master's study, I decided to create a project that would address the problem I was most disturbed and affected by: race. Living in a city divided by two sides of the tracks, I thought there was an opportunity to have influence. This naive, arrogant, white do-gooder set out to design a set of interventions that would change racial attitudes created by more than 100 years of history. I believed if I simply brought people together, they would have a Kumbaya moment and all would be well. To make matters even more challenging, I decided to prove my hypothesis with a group of adolescents!

First, I brought a Black history professor into my Sunday school class, only to hear responses like, "Our ancestors took good care of our slaves" and "We aren't responsible for our white kin, and we don't want to hear this anymore. The Civil War is over!" Wow, did I get the education that I desperately needed. Who was I, a white, privileged Yankee, to come in and start pointing out what these folks needed to change?

I also created a youth choir, bringing together black and white singers to perform together. I visited numerous churches to gather a group of white middle- and highschoolers, but only eight children out of the entire community were allowed to participate. I was crestfallen but determined; eventually, 250 black kids and eight soul-filled white kids performed together. The concert was life-changing for me, for them, and for all those who attended. They sang with such heart, and I will never forget the joy in the faces of not just 258 kids but also their parents!

My final attempt to change the racial attitudes was to re-write an existing rock opera, add choreography, and take the kids from our church to Florida. They stayed in homeless shelters and church basements in diverse areas, and they met kids from all different backgrounds. It was transformative, and many of them developed a new perspective about the beliefs that had been passed on to them. They began to choose a different way of recognizing and appreciating others who didn't look like them or live like them. It was a bold move on my part, and if it were not for the incredible support of the parents who made it happen, none of these programs would have succeeded. I am so grateful that they trusted me and allowed me to introduce their children to a different world.

My learning about cultural bias went both ways. I, too, was biased, racist, prejudiced, judgmental, and whatever other critical words can be used to describe a passionate, privileged white woman trying to change a major socially embedded belief that had existed for generations. Now I recognize that I had a sense of moral courage that at times was definitely "holier than thou." However, the outcome of my efforts and the support from the members of that very special community connected us for life. I am still in contact with some of the teens and their parents, and they will always hold a special place in my heart.

WOMEN'S RIGHTS

My identity was challenged not only by racism but also by feminism (or the lack thereof). The first time someone called me Reverend Mrs., I was in shock. I didn't know what to say. A liberal feminist from New England given a title based on her husband's job wasn't going to fly with me.

There were regular gatherings for ministers and their wives—back then, all heterosexual couples. Even using this language of "ministers and their wives" feels so incorrect to me, but remember, it was the '80s. We would put on our church attire, me in a dress (and of course nylons, despite the hot weather) and Will in his suit and tie, and visit different regional churches. The men, the preachers, would adjourn to their study while the women, their wives, went to the parlor. (Yes, women ministers were starting to appear then, but it was still men on one side and women on the other when it came to church power and leadership.)

There was a cultural dilemma for me. My East Coast feminist background left me bewildered about how and why women would repeatedly choose to take a secondary role in church leadership. It wasn't until later, reflecting on my sensibilities and biases, that I realized they were not doing that. Feminism is about women making choices. Their choices may not have been mine, but they played vital roles in the church community, and just because I didn't make the same choice didn't mean they were wrong. But back then, I wasn't okay with their lifestyle, and again tried to change them. When the wives planned to put together a cookbook to raise money, I challenged the idea with something I considered more intellectually stimulating: holding a feminist theology conference. The blank stares made me want to sink into the ground. How was I ever going to make this life work?

Like many women before me, the answer that came to me was to start a family. Isn't that what we are expected to do after marriage? Have a child? Of course! That is what everyone does! We were no exception in wanting to start our own family. That was our goal, but for some reason, it was not so easy for me. Try as we did, I was not getting pregnant, and my sense of inadequacy was wreaking havoc on my confidence.

REFLECTION QUESTIONS

1. Have you ever lived in a place where you felt out of place?
2. Have you ever been in situations when your values didn't fit?
3. What helped you accept other points of view?

CHAPTER 15

THE LOSS OF MY CHILD

An opportunity arose for us to move back to New England to pastor a church in a small town in Maine. We took the spot in the hopes that it would be helpful to us as individuals and as a couple.

If you have never visited Maine, just imagine a well-worn road flanked by large trees cascading bright hues of orange and red on either side like a canopy of color. That was early fall where we lived. It was also the time when farmers were completing their pumpkin harvest and preparing their fields for the winter snow that was soon to arrive.

One day soon after our move, I woke up nauseous and feeling like I hadn't even slept. My chest was hurting, and I started to wonder to myself, *"Am I? Could I be?"* Yes, I was pregnant. Nothing bothered me—I was on a hormonal high. This baby was my everything, and every move I made was for him or her. Our excitement was infectious, and members of the community began to congratulate us. It was even more wonderful that the baby would be born here, closer to my parents and best friends. I was elated.

A few weeks later, on a brisk fall day, I was gazing out at the garden behind our modest A-frame house. I imagined that garden in the springtime when the flowers would dance with color in the wind. I imagined carrying my newborn baby into that garden to marvel at the rainbow of colors.

I had a sudden urge to plant red tulips. I wanted to make the image of my baby and me looking at tulips a reality. Donning my down jacket and gloves, I found the gardening tools, located the bulbs, and took them outside. Despite the changing weather—the wind was howling and the temperature dropping fast—I was determined to get those bulbs into the ground at that moment. I dug into the earth and quickly placed the bulbs inside, tenderly saying a prayer over each one. It was like a ritual, and I couldn't stop. Disregarding the worsening weather and frigid cold, I felt something telling me that I needed to say that little prayer for each future tulip.

When the last bulb was planted and I made my way to the front door, I felt a sharp pain in my stomach—cramping that caused me to double over. Grabbing my stomach, I moved inside and sat down in the large recliner we had in the study. I thought to myself, *Surely it's just part of pregnancy. I'll lay down and it will go away.* But it didn't. I started asking myself questions and remembered waking up that day feeling unusually well, with no morning sickness. I had dismissed the change then; now I realized I might need help.

I called Sarah, a nurse friend, and asked her to meet me at the women's clinic where I was being cared for. She readily agreed.

I am so thankful that my friend came that day. Will was delayed. Sitting in the ultrasound room with my legs apart and my feet gently placed in the stirrups, I needed someone with me. The technician, a young twenty-something, came in, and without uttering a word began to insert the orb inside me. Within a minute, she gasped and said, "Oh no, I need to get the doctor, I'll be right back."

The technician burst out of the room. Being a nurse, sweet Sarah probably knew before me, but I had to wait agonizing minutes before a physician came in and told me my baby was dead.

The next hours were a heartbreaking blur of tears. I remember being wheeled into a basement exam room where I had to wait almost 30 minutes by myself before receiving a D&C. Of course, the staff there—the nurses, the assistants, everyone—was kind and loving and extended that pitiful look that still makes me cringe when I think of it.

Miscarriage is a confusing loss, especially when it occurs during the first trimester. Instead of acknowledging the loss of someone's dream of motherhood, you hear a lot of "This happens a lot, you will be fine, and you will get pregnant again." The only people who knew what to say were women who had gone through the same experience. A woman in her eighties sent me a note. She described a ritual she created every Mother's Day to remember the children she had lost.

Children? Could this happen again? Surely not! I wasn't even going to entertain the thought.

REFLECTION QUESTIONS

1. Has a major loss ever come unexpectedly in your life?
2. If so, how did you manage your grief?
3. What one lesson have you learned that you most want to remember the next time you face loss?

CHAPTER 16

◆—◆—◆

FINDING MY VOICE

In the days after the miscarriage, I took long walks with Sarah, and she was one of the few who understood the pain of my loss. This was even more evident on a day when some strangers came to my door.

The dining room table was still set up for an afternoon tea I had scheduled before the pregnancy loss. The china settings with their dainty pink roses and gold trim were set up exactly the way my etiquette handbook told me to place them. The polished silver was placed precisely beside the china on top of the pure white linen tablecloths washed and pressed to perfection. At that time in my life, in my mind my role as hostess and minister's wife was tied to my ability to nurture my guests with presence and style and a welcoming table; I was a Martha Stewart wannabe.

I had canceled the tea and hadn't had many visitors recently; the people from our congregation were honoring our request and need for privacy. I was surprised to see a dark Cadillac coming down our driveway. A young couple I did not recognize shuffled down the driveway and came to my door. They introduced themselves as church visitors from another state. Living in a parsonage and serving as a minister's spouse, it was not unusual for me to receive people visiting from other places. When someone was traveling, they frequently stopped in for an informal friendly visit. Grateful that my formal table was still prepared, I welcomed them in and dutifully led them to the dining room, offered them refreshments, and explained my husband was not available. Despite my current physical and mental health, I disguised my vulnerability. June Cleaver could not have done better.

After a polite exchange of pleasantries, I found myself explaining my loss and sharing why I was home on a weekday. The gentleman asked me how long it had been, and when I said two weeks, his response startled me. "Two weeks is ample time for you and your husband to get back to work; after all, it was only a miscarriage." His wife, barely old enough to be married and have a family, supported his view, telling me that my job was ministry and to "support your husband's flock." She said that it was time to put it behind me and get back to work. I, like my husband, had a church to serve. The anger that came from my ovaries to my face was lethal.

I listened as long as I could and then spoke. "As the only woman here who lost a child, I would like to speak. You have no right to tell me when I am ready to resume anything!"

With a patronizing tone that dripped from every word, the man said, "Now, we know you have been through a lot, but you must trust us: you aren't thinking straight. The Lord is guiding us, and we know what's best." I stood up abruptly and told them, "Please leave my house." When they didn't move fast enough, I moved forward, gesturing them out the door. As they drove away, I winged one of those teacups against the wall. It was my way of rebelling against the china-doll expectation of women to be vulnerable and fragile and in need of a man's guidance. In that moment, I was fierce, not fragile!

I was expressing the same kind of feminine rage my mother had when she hit me. My anger wasn't toward this couple; it was much more intense and greater than that moment. It was built-up frustration from all the times I felt unheard and misunderstood and told to be better, stronger, prettier, wiser, more of a woman, etc. My feminine role was once again being challenged, and I was hearing "You aren't enough. You are letting others down." That was, of course, not their intention, but well-meaning people often make triggering statements during times of loss out of love and discomfort. This was one of those times.

After the two unsuspecting strangers had left, I felt wholly inadequate. I understood the truest meaning of the word *barren*: empty, void of purpose, worthless. Alone with my toxic translations of their words, I was lost. In my exhaustion, I found myself ruminating on the idea that "Christian women are supposed to have God-given strength to give birth and to rise up and serve in any circumstance." Yet my body was still feeling the symptoms of pregnancy combined with pain from the D&C, my soul still weeping, and my heart was broken at the loss of a dream. I wasn't ready to stand up and pretend I was strong and faithful.

The conflict was unbearable. There is a loneliness that sinks in and defies words when your faith—the beliefs that guide your every move and choice, the very foundation of your identity—fails you. It is profound and requires every bit of your spiritual muscles to garner the strength to rise up.

Like many of the people I have worked with, especially women with self-esteem issues, I tended to go from one extreme to another, from intimidated to intimidating. Eventually, I would realize that there was a happy medium, a more compassionate approach. I now understand that I can be assertive without being aggressive; the choice is not between being intimidated or intimidating. So perhaps I could have been less aggressive on that day while still asserting my right to speak. But there is one thing I will not be in such a moment: silent.

To lift yourself up, you must find your voice. When facing loss, you have to draw on the spiritual muscles that exist within all of us: they will give you the strength to voice your needs. When loss brought me to my knees, literally, I stood up and found my voice by sitting back down.

That teacup was my feminine rage rising up, my desperate desire to be enough, and my awareness of choice. I didn't have to listen to anyone else's thoughts. I could choose to hear my own voice. In that moment, my rage woke me up, and I heard the still, small voice of unconditional love. The wise woman inside of me told me *how to take care of me.*

God doesn't ask us to self-sacrifice! We can't be of service if we don't honor ourselves as precious. I found my invincible belief, a truth that aligned with my interpretation of faith. I remembered the shortest verse in the Bible: "Jesus wept." I recognized, acknowledged, and honored my grief, which had no timeline. Others could wait. My self-care mattered. In that moment, I lifted myself up by allowing myself to sink into a chair, rest, and grieve.

REFLECTION QUESTIONS

1. Have you managed conflicts with those who dismiss who you are?
2. Do you remember a time when you felt dismissed or unheard, and you lost your voice?
3. What one thing can you remember with which to lift yourself up when you start feeling small?

CHAPTER 17

LETTING GO OF THE REINS

My renewed sense of strength meant that it was time for me to regroup and re-create myself once again. I needed to return to the path I felt called to follow: *my* path. Guided by what I had learned from my first luminary, Jason, I re-discovered my passion and purpose: to create uplifting communities of care for dying children and their parents. After the death of my child, this passion became a raging fire. But how to move forward?

Jason's death left me with a hole not only in my heart but in my life. What was my next step? I had a promise to fulfill that I did not take lightly! Where would I start? What did Jason represent to me? Who did he most want me to help? How did meeting him fit with the call to create children's hospice programs? While I reflected on this, I remembered something Jason said to me: "I want them to know that no matter what happens, there is help, they aren't alone."

Who was the "them" he referred to? And then I knew: kids. Sick kids. Dying kids.

Thus began my divine purpose: to create communities of care around people in need, beginning with dying children.

In her biography, Quest, The Life of Elisabeth Kübler-Ross by Derek Gill, Elisabeth says that gathering an understanding of the complexity of as many social and psychological issues as possible is essential in providing excellent care at end-of-life I knew I needed to ground myself in a combination of medical, emotional, and spiritual influences on human behavior and bring all the aspects of humanity together in my approach to this work.

I also knew that Jason would be a part of this next step in my life. If I was to help dying kids and their parents, I needed to find a place where I could combine Jason's story and my own with the learning that Elisabeth called for. Antioch New England Graduate School was that place. I applied and was accepted into a doctoral program in psychology.

Determined to follow my designated path, I self-selected children and families as an area of focus and found myself writing down my goal of working with dying children in every class. They were my inspiration. Every paper and every class was influenced by my desire to learn as much as I could about this targeted population. When my advisor, Cathy Lerner, and I began discussing the topic of my dissertation, Jason's story was all she had to hear. "That has to be your dissertation," she told me. "Tell his story and design a model of care based on what you learned." My dissertation— "Looking Through Both Sides of a Window: An Adolescent Living Unto Death"—was born that day. It would eventually be the foundation of the Jason Program.

At Antioch, I was building the future, finding the path to achieving what I wanted to do with the rest of my life. At home, however, our planned future was unraveling, dissipating, and becoming empty. Still reeling from the loss of my child and the insensitive and overbearing attitude of the visiting strangers, I decided to take advantage of a break from school and go to a place far away—a place where I could rediscover that Vermont version of Anne of Green Gables I once was: that little girl who escaped to wherever she could be alone and hear nature's whispers.

I heard about a riding program in Wyoming, and I knew that the vast canyons and rolling foothills of the Wind River Mountains would be the sanctuary I was seeking. I longed to be surrounded by nothing but wide-open skies and pastures. I wanted to feel the wind at my back as I rode over gopher holes and passed by the fences that marked the only division of the land. I wanted to watch the cattle graze peacefully. A sense of unending potential and power emanated from the rich dust of the prairie. There, I could be me, not someone's wife, not someone's Reverend Mrs., not anyone else's anything: just me and the twisting tumbleweed.

It was a cool morning under a cobalt blue sky on the plains of Montana.

I was riding a horse named M&M with a group herding horses across 250 miles. After a few hours, suddenly I spotted a dark, majestic, powerful presence standing erect on the top face of one of the hills. My heart stopped. It is rare to see a black stallion in the wild, but there he was, ready to steer any of our mares away from the herd to join him. Female horses instinctively follow the male leader, and our guide understood this natural law because he immediately screamed, "Hold them back!" As if on cue, our herd horses began to fly, dodging the sagebrush instinctively as they pounded toward the stallion—followed closely by the horses we were riding. It took every ounce of strength for us to hold on to our reins. Many of us grabbed onto the horn at the top of the saddle to steady ourselves and stay on. They were in charge, for regardless of our strength, these animals outweighed and outpowered us.

I gathered my strength, reaching out to grab the mountain face and steady myself as we flew past it, moving my handkerchief over my mouth to stop the dust from streaming into my mouth. Sweat poured down my face, and the smell of horse sweat and my own reminded me of the sixteen-year-old girl who would take chances and place herself in the hands of Mother Nature, believing that repeating to myself "Just hold on and keep going" would somehow keep me safe. The horse blanket slipping, the girth widening, my heart racing, I clung to those words as tightly as my legs gripped the horse's body.

Finally, our guide called out: "Give it up!" and we followed the guide into a canyon where our horses could no longer see the dark male and the six mares from our herd who were now in his power. We came to a full stop by a watering hole. Petting our equine partners, we began to share our stories about dodging this and making it over that, and we were so caught up in re-living the experience that none of us noticed that our guide had no idea where we were.

Our group, once connected in the desire to outrun our nemesis, now became divided between those too tired to continue and those willing to try and outrun the sun and find camp. Our guide decided to stay with those who were unable to move. The rest of us made sure our horses were watered and set off on our own, led by our companions into the desert with the burnt orange sky slowly darkening on the horizon.

My horse was the last to get water, and I tried to call out to the others to let them know I couldn't keep up. Galloping over the thorny bushes, I felt the scrapes on my chaps as my horse and I headed out as quickly as we could, trying to outrun the sunset. The burning blisters between my legs paled in comparison to the frantic beating of my heart as I tried and tried to get the attention of those ahead of me, but as my smaller horse began to slow down, the figures of my team faded, and all I could see was distant dust kicked up into the failing light.

Suddenly my horse, M&M, became still. Here we were with nothing in sight but the velvety black sky. Having no sense of direction and with no dwelling or light in sight, I did what I was taught to do when I was a little girl growing up in Vermont lost in the woods: I prayed. "Now what do I do?" Then I stopped crying long enough to hear the answer. It came as if sung out as loud as the hard breathing of my exhausted horse: *Let go of the reins.*

Trusting myself and this animal, I released my grip and tied the reins carefully around the horn. Adjusting myself to center completely on top of the withers, I took a deep breath, kicked with all my strength, and allowed this partnership to become a leadership: My horse would lead me to safety.

Swiftly, she leaped forward, jumping with her agile legs 180 degrees, and took off into the dark. Letting go of the reins meant entrusting my life to a being I barely knew, but as she snorted and gained speed and moved with such grace, rising and falling over the mounds of this rugged terrain, I felt that I was in the best of those 14 hands.

It felt as if I had been riding blindfolded for 20 minutes, but suddenly there they were: we had caught up with the others, now close enough for them to hear me bellow, "Help! Help!" They stopped, some bursting into tears realizing I was safe. They had noticed me missing but chose to keep going toward camp so they could drive back in a jeep with bright headlights that could pierce the darkness. Once again, heading off toward nowhere, we allowed the horses to be our guides. The animals were the reliable ones, the ones we could trust to get us back to where we needed to be. After more excruciatingly exhausting minutes, the red spotlight of the lanterns hanging in the mess tent of our camp shone in the distance, and our horses followed that beacon.

We dismounted in front of our tents, and I felt a gentle touch around my waist: a male friend was reaching out to hold me as I fell to the ground.

He stretched out his hand, understanding I could barely walk on my own. I realized in that moment what it felt like to be fully vulnerable, not having to play a role to act strong. I knew that my life had changed forever. I wasn't meant to be a minister's wife. I had my own ministry—my own skills, gifts, talents, and messages to share. *This* was church. These strangers were teaching me how to surround someone experiencing loss with community. I wasn't supposed to show as a minister's wife that I wasn't "strong." I shared the responsibility for not getting my needs met, and what I learned from letting go of the reins is that allowing yourself to be vulnerable is the only way for people to help you.

And I knew at that moment that I wanted something different. I was reminded of my calling—that voice that spoke to me on the bench in college. It was time for me to follow my own path. This was one of those road-less-taken moments. I was going to choose to leave a marriage—not because my husband was unkind, but because he needed someone different to be a minister's wife. And I needed someone to support me in my form of ministry. A little pinto named M&M had shown me that I deserved to follow my dreams wholeheartedly.

One of the fundamental lessons to learn as you struggle to lift yourself up from loss is to let go. It takes faith that things will be all right: that you will be lifted and lit up. Faith can be religious, but it can also mean just letting go of the reins (figuratively, or in my case literally) and trusting the future. Letting go of what no longer works can open the space for something new and better. And that has certainly proved to be true in my life.

A minister's wife once said to me after she had ended her marriage, "Life is wonderful, but new life, even better." I never forgot those words of comfort. They gave me the kind of courage Jason called "have to," and I repeat them as often as I can to anyone who is making that choice.

After my divorce from Will, I met the man who would become my second husband. I cannot tell you how important John has been to my life. He is my partner, soul mate, and the one who finishes the lyrics to my song when I have forgotten the words. He became my lifeline as I began drafting my dissertation and bringing Jason's legacy and my promise to him to life. Without John, I could never have accomplished what I was about to do.

REFLECTION QUESTIONS

1. What do you think of when you hear the term "letting go?"
2. When have you struggled with this concept?
3. What is one thing you can do to support yourself when you need to let go?

CHAPTER 18

THE JASON PROGRAM

Support from John gave me the courage and strength to fulfill my promise to Jason and create his legacy. My dissertation, "Looking Through Both Sides of a Window: An Adolescent Living Unto Death," included an interview I had with Jason and his mother, Timmie, about his dying experience. In giving me the interview, Jason said, "I want my legacy to be for anyone who thinks giving up is easier than going on with their fight, to be a learning experience for others, to teach them how to go on, to tell others how I got through it through prayer, stories of faith, and maintaining a positive attitude. That helps me."

The following is a transcript of the interview.

Katie: What is a positive attitude?

Jason: Never worry because if you worry about it and it doesn't happen, you worry for nothing. If it does happen, you have experienced the pain twice.

K: What helps you maintain a positive attitude?

J: Going on as normally as possible. People didn't change to fit around me. When I went to school bald, they dealt with it. Girls would pat me on the head and look for my brain.

K: How did you react to your peers?

J: I had to set an example, be a leader. People would notice me more; therefore, I had to make a positive statement.

K: Did you ever feel insecure?

J: No.

Timmie: The greatest gift you can give your child is a positive self-image.

J: I didn't allow cancer to change me. I had to grow up faster and I took less for granted.

K: What do you mean, not taking life for granted?

J: Life is worth a lot more than people think it is. When life comes to the point where it may stop, you take it less for granted.

K: What about the idea you may die?

Timmie: We are all dying. If people would prepare themselves, it can be a beautiful experience. Take the time to share feelings and live each day.

Jason: It's there, but you don't have to think about it if you have peace of mind.

K: What would you miss most if you died in a month?

J: Getting married and having kids.

K: What is most helpful for you?

J: Money. It allows me to give to other people. I wish I had a million dollars to give to people for transportation, food, and education. People who bring food and say, "How are you feeling?" instead of "How are you?" People who aren't afraid to kiss and hug.

K: What is least helpful?

J: People who ask questions about what they don't understand. Making conversation out of their own discomfort. Get beyond the small talk.

Inspired by these words and studying children's hospice movements just beginning across the country, I formed the idea that if we could provide families with medical, emotional, and spiritual support along with meeting their practical daily living needs through volunteers, we could truly make a difference.

This general goal coalesced into a specific plan: forming a non-profit organization to support seriously ill children and their families. Jason's legacy became the Jason Program.

I now had a vision and a way of executing it; it was time to sell the idea.

The first place I decided to share my plan outside of my safe school setting was at a party with a state advocate for children. A friend had invited me knowing I had this vision and that this person would be there. Garnering the courage Jason called "have to," I approached a middle-aged, well-dressed individual and proceeded to describe my passion for providing support to seriously ill and dying children in Maine. Their first reaction was not at all what I expected.

"Kids don't die in Maine!"

"Excuse me," I responded, "Did you just say kids don't die here?"

This compassionate, well-meaning soul went on to say that this kind of program was not necessary because we had great programs to keep kids alive and there was no need for it.

Stunned at the ignorance and the naivety of this response, I thanked them and went away deep in thought. I had learned from working in a hospice and with churches that every bit of information from potential stakeholders was important to heed in developing any kind of program. A child advocate had just given me important feedback. I needed to speak at one of those programs that miraculously kept all children alive.

Thankfully, I heard about a seminar hosted by the Maine Hospice Council about caring for dying children. Just under the deadline, I was accepted as a speaker. Little did I know that I would meet the core of the Jason Program team that day.

As I began to present my idea of a community-based hospice-like team, a young, short pediatric oncologist sitting in front of me started scribbling notes non-stop. I convinced myself he wasn't listening to me; he had to catch up on his charting. I was wrong. When I approached Dr. Gary Allegretta after the presentation, he told me that he loved my ideas and was interested in talking more, although that day he had to rush off.

That same day, I met an RN named Greg Burns, a young, energetic, loveable guy with a smile that lit up the room. Greg has a perfect personality for working with kids. We chatted informally and he, too, said he liked some of my ideas. Then Greg, like Gary, needed to rush off to patients waiting to be seen.

Finally, I met a social worker named Deb Donelson who worked for the local hospital's oncology program. She wanted to talk about her work with sick kids who sometimes die. That would be the beginning of an amazing friendship with someone who is a kindred spirit and with whom I have shared my love of this work for many years. Deb became a great teacher, helping me understand the complexities of presenting the concept that children die when most people want to focus on how to help them live.

Here lies the ultimate dilemma in the world of children's hospice: How do you get people to fund a program that admits to having failed to cure a child? There had to be a way to express the message of living unto death: It was not about how long they lived but how they lived until they died.

As I did many times throughout my life, I silently and reverently asked for guidance, hoping to hear that voice. And I did. *"Remember Jason's story!"* it said. In an instant, I recalled a community of caring individuals supporting him in living until death, and it hit me that there was the pitch: *Living until they died.* And where was Jason's community? Church. I needed to go to the churches.

So, to the churches I went, and in one of those churches, I met Mary Lee Wile, an Episcopal lay priest, in an interfaith ministry meeting. Her energy, kindness, and loving spirit drew me to her immediately. It was natural for me to share my vision with her. As with Gary and Greg, Mary Lee didn't hesitate to want to help. A team was emerging, and together we launched the Jason Program.

I often get asked, "How can you watch children die?" Watching them die is not as difficult as watching adults who could have helped those children deny them what they needed to live until they died.

I remember sitting at a fundraiser with some very wealthy potential donors. Despite the fact that they were there to support our program, when I mentioned that these kids died, a woman attendee literally turned her back to me and started a new conversation. And then there was the group who refused to support us because we were "too sad." I have too many examples of how people turned away from our mission, but fortunately, there were many, many more who understood and supported us and, more importantly, the kids.

Over and over there was resistance to acknowledging that kids die, which is why building the program around the children instead of vice versa worked. Their wisdom, as Jason had shown me, was the wind beneath my wings. Every time an adult resisted my idea, I took a deep breath and remembered the children: their challenges, their spirits, and most importantly, their teachings. And then some people showed up believing in my purpose-driven passion—like Louise Hay. At the workshop where I first met her, she gave me sage advice: "When in doubt, Katie, ask the kids!" I never forgot her wisdom, and it means so much to me that I am publishing this book with a company she helped create. I know she would be pleased.

Next up, let me introduce you to some of these inspiring luminaries. You will never forget them.

REFLECTION QUESTIONS

1. Have you ever had an idea that you passionately believed in and others rejected?
2. How did you handle the rejection?
3. Were you able to discover your champions, the helpers who validated your idea?

PART 3
THE WISDOM OF CHILDREN

Listen to the children, they will show you how to love,
Listen to the children, they will show you how to live..."
                    —"Listen to the Children," a song by Katie Eastman

We are all born with a spiritual knowing that we belong to and have been created to contribute to bettering this world. We see this knowledge in all children, who are very much focused on the here and now—what is right in front of them. Their needs are food, water, love, and a sense of connection and belonging. As they get older, fears and insecurities develop from the outside influences of the world, and they become less focused on these fundamental human needs.

Dying children, however, are removed from these influences, and in a sense brought back to this core understanding of what it is to be human. This is why they can be present and offer a compassionate focus to their relationships. The dying children I knew taught me about how important it was to open my heart to the "other." Each one of them, regardless of their limitations, possessed a way of caring that superseded their challenges. They loved despite their limits. As philosopher and author Ken Wilber once explained to me, dying children are so beautifully compassionate because they are closer to birth. This vulnerable state allows their soul's voice to be heard and leads them to be open-hearted warriors: to shine light and create ripples of compassion.

Elisabeth Kübler-Ross wrote about this in her book, *A Letter to a Child with Cancer.* It was inspired by and written for Dougie, a young boy with cancer who asked her to explain why children die. In the book, Elisabeth described the story of birth and rebirth in nature. She wrote that all of nature reminds us that life is not permanent; the only aspect of life that is certain is the cycle of change when things die, offering opportunities for new growth and life. Children are not immune to that part of the cycle, so they experience change and sometimes death.

Elisabeth ultimately reminded Dougie that it's not how long you live; it's how you live that matters. Dougie then turned to Elisabeth to help him and his family live until his death. Dougie rode his bike; Dougie played; Dougie enjoyed his family and as many aspects of living as he could; he made a difference and contributed to the world. Grieving centers in his name exist throughout the globe, places where children receive support to continue to be childlike while sharing their painful losses. They offer these children a space to heal.

The dying children I write about in this book followed the same pattern of living until they died and offering life lessons about what is truly important. That's why I call them luminaries; during their short lives, they enlightened everyone in their presence. These wise luminaries knew something that the rest of us must learn and relearn throughout our lives: what it is like to live our highest and best life, attending to and directing our energies to what is most important: food, water, love, and belonging.

As human beings, our arrival into this world is the beginning of a lifetime of trying to engage with what Andrew Cohen calls our "evolutionary impulses," which draw us back to the simplicity of caring about ourselves and each other—a state children understand innately. It's our unlearning of these basics that we spend a lifetime repairing. We all once had the same wisdom as the luminaries, but over time we lose our childlike faith and understanding and spend a lifetime trying to return to the innocent sense of knowing we once held. Anyone blessed to know a luminary is never the same. We learn from them that we are only limited by our misguided perspectives or beliefs. Once we can break free of those self-limiting perspectives, we are ready to accept better alternatives.

In this section, you will meet six luminaries as well as four pairs of mothers and children who teamed up to teach me about the depth of that connection. We'll also touch on the losses of suicide and abortion.

Remember Austin's conversation with his mom just before he died? You are about to learn more about what he meant when he said, "You knew, but you grew up."

CHAPTER 19

AUSTIN: "THERE ARE ANGELS EVERYWHERE"

Each of the luminaries you'll meet in this section captured one of the sources of light that combine to build the indomitable spiritual muscle that made them so much stronger and wiser than us able-bodied adults.

Austin, the luminary who spoke his truth in the beginning of this book, was one of my most formidable and wisest teachers, and he was only eight years old. The light Austin showed to the world was the light of love.

There he was, perched on the porch overlooking the vast field. His parrot calmly rested on his shoulder as I approached his mother; her long dark hair and athletic body and welcoming smile invited me to sit. She described Austin's cancer diagnosis and the last few years of chemotherapy and regular trips to the hospital—the sleepless nights, the struggles to get childcare for her younger child, Brian, then a toddler. Gazing down at the wooden steps that led from the porch to the field a few feet away, she went on to plead for help with his physical and emotional pain. He was a 7-year-old living a monastery-like existence who desperately wanted to live, his anger palpable whenever he talked about what was happening to him.

My first visit to Austin was like many that followed. I sat next to him in the Adirondack rocker on the porch overlooking the calm green meadow that stood in contrast with Austin's fiery response to his cancer. Austin taught a very important lesson with a vital message: *question everything!*

"Why me, why am I dying?" he would ask. "I want to understand *why*. Where is faith? This isn't fair. Why me? Why? I don't want to die!"

Austin challenged me with those questions. There is no better teacher about not faking or trying to dismiss a question than a pre-teen. They can smell fake. So, I was very thoughtful and contemplative myself. I silently asked for guidance from my tender loving core. I remembered the sage words from graduate school: "Listen more, speak less, don't tell them answers but value their questions." These words echoed in my thoughts incessantly.

I knew there needed to be a source of connection, a way for us to come together and share on whatever level Austin needed. He had a labyrinth in his backyard, a circular pathway filled with carefully placed beach stones he had gathered near his home. Austin led me there and I followed, taking in every detail of what he was showing me. He slowly ambled toward it. It was like watching him struggle for answers, witnessing him stumble and collect himself but keep moving forward to this remarkable symbolic expression of his contemplative nature.

He asked me what I thought of it. Speechless at its size and its location in the back of a home close to suburbia, I found myself struggling to respond. I asked him if it was all right if I walked with him around the circle. He readily agreed. Each rounded section held a different story for Austin. As we entered, he recalled his diagnosis and recounted with me what he felt when he was told by his physician, "You have cancer." *A gut punch* is what he said. He described the ensuing treatments, trips away from home, time away from school, and the challenges he had met during that time.

The next circle seemed to be the place where he recalled the impact of his cancer on others. He talked about watching his mother cry. He told me about his brother's unease whenever he was in pain and his disappointment when Austin couldn't get down on the floor and play. He expressed gratitude for community members and how much their support meant to him and what he wanted to ensure that everyone knew: he wanted them to continue like the labyrinth circles, never taking a moment of life for granted. It frustrated him that anyone could miss a moment of enjoying their life.

The final circle seemed to reflect where he was in his life, living in the moment where he asked profound existential questions about what it all meant. Here, he challenged me to speak. He would not settle for me throwing the question back at him. He wanted to push me to make my own philosophical beliefs known. Thankfully, I had studied faith from the time I was very young from the perspective of honoring the questions. Here, I was faced with a Buddha-like, wise soul, challenging me to define what I hadn't wanted to define.

So, here is what I said: "Austin, I don't have answers about the reality of why children die, or why there is pain and suffering. Those questions are left for me and you to wonder about. But I do have a solid answer about what we are meant to do because of it. My faith tells me to show up with love amid all the horrible and unfair things that happen. I and the flowers and your bird and your family and your friends and your community and every living being that comes near you are sending you love. Simple to say when I am not the one dying, and yet that's all I've got, Austin. Love and compassion and caring and support. Whatever you think you need, we will do our best to make sure you get it." We agreed at that moment that I would keep showing up and asking him what he needed, and he would tell me.

As time progressed, he sought answers to more questions about the existence of God. He hoped that by finding spiritual answers, he could make peace with death.

Austin didn't make peace with death. He fought to the end to cling to life and living. That was what made him Austin—his determination to remain whole and strong as his body weakened. He was filled with faith and fortitude.

We do not have to stop asking profound spiritual questions, but we must also not rest in the answers. The labyrinth is a symbolic reminder that each time we walk around it, life has changed. Each new day, life offers us new opportunities to challenge ourselves. Austin, at an incredibly early age, understood this. He rose to each daily challenge with thoughtful determination.

I ran a marathon several years ago, and as I ran one of the miles, I thought of him. His memory carried me over the steepest hill with ease as I remembered his strength. His mother once told me that caring for him was like running a daily marathon. With his intensity and profound strength, keeping up with him and his symbolic daily walk around the labyrinth must have been both exhausting from the daily increasing number of losses as much as it was exhilarating with the number of lessons.

He lived at home until he died, and he received visitors, classmates, and community members. Many would walk with him through the labyrinth. When he could no longer walk and became bedridden, his spirit began to change. Three days before he died, he delivered one of the most important statements I have ever heard in my life. It bears repeating.

Austin turned to his mom, who was in his room adjusting the curtains to allow the sun to come in and shine on him.

Mom?
Yes, what's up, Bud?
I have something to tell you and I hope you tell everyone in the world because it is important.
What is it?
There is love all around, and angels on earth and Heaven are the same. And Mom, the purpose of life is to make a difference.
Austin, how did you know that, and I didn't?
You knew all this, Mom, when you were little, but you forgot when you grew up.

Wow! Out of the mouths of… Not only was his mother stunned by this wisdom, but everyone who has heard it since shares in the mystery of how he knew it. Who told him this? Did he hear a voice? How was it communicated to him? Anyone who knows his story and has shared the gift he gave us has been touched by the power of this lesson. This boy, brought to the world for such a short life, had a heartfelt understanding of what is most important and a personality that made us think about it. This little prophet had a mission, and he fulfilled it. He enlightened many with his mystic sense of wonder, and it was fitting that when he took his last breath, a burst of light shone through his bedroom window.

There is light in the dark, and it is in the form of love and compassion. Austin taught me that.

REFLECTION QUESTION:

1. What do you think of Austin's quote?
2. Can you relate to Austin's optimistic view of the world? To his frustration?
3. If you were Austin's mother, how would you have responded to his declaration?

CHAPTER 20

WALDEN: THE UPSIDE-DOWN RAINBOW

The inner wisdom children are born with can show up in the most unexpected places and in the smallest of beings. Like an upside-down rainbow, it can catch us off guard and surprise us with its uplifting strength. Nobody proved that better than Walden, the youngest of my luminaries.

§

We gathered by the center of town, people of all ages, to honor a life born too soon. He weighed only a few pounds, but his spirit was vast and expansive.

Walden, a premature infant, had been brought home to live and die surrounded by his extended family and his community, with his tiniest of hearts beating against the odds.

Yet he brought so much perspective to the daily life of all of us who knew him and his precious family. On that day, his grandparents, mom and dad, and a full community of admirers came to honor Walden with a walk around the community. They, like me, had marveled at the strength it must have taken for this little boy, whose head fit into the palm of your hand, to keep going.

Inspired by him and his family and the outpouring of love he drew to him, many people described how they would live their lives differently because of Walden's inspiration. The ripple of compassion that emanated from one little soul was unimaginable. And then the day we honored him became even more magical: we looked into the sky and there before us was an upside-down rainbow. His mother, Allison, motioned to me. "Kate, look up! Can you see it?" and there it was, as if Walden was sending us his smile in the sky above us.

There were tears of loss and smiles of joy, and in that moment, I understood a fundamental lesson of life: that amid loss, there are upside-down rainbows: moments where amid unimaginable pain, if we pay attention, we can hear or feel or see evidence of the ripple of compassion, love, light, and tenderness that can surround even the most difficult of losses. That day, we were symbolically reminded that if we keep going, there will appear a rainbow of some kind—a message of hope, a loving gesture, a presence that will reassure us that someday, things will get better.

Walden's short but powerful life exemplified how loss and hope, two contrasting dynamics, can coexist, just like an upside-down rainbow. Walden inspired us to believe that we as human beings are capable of so much more than we know. Within us is a strength that surpasses our understanding. How could someone so frail lift up and light up so many with his strength?

Walden's photo sits on my desk as a reminder that there are examples of upside-down rainbows everywhere. Hope shows itself in ways we could easily miss if we aren't paying attention. Walden will always represent to me that sometimes we find inspiration in the tiniest vessels. Our heroes and sheroes don't have to be big famous adults; they can be tiny hearts capable of generating enormous love.

Walden possessed an energy, a light, a powerful love like the wind that lifts the geese with the support of the V. Walden showed us that we all have some voice inside that gives us the strength we need to access in a moment of struggle. I grew to understand this as spiritual muscles. He lifted us up with the lightest of spirits and the strongest of hearts.

REFLECTION QUESTIONS

1. What does the image of an upside-down rainbow represent for you?
2. Why do you think Walden impacted so many people?
3. Is there a time when you discovered hope when you were tired and ready to give up?

CHAPTER 21

MARIA: "I'LL SEE YOU IN HEAVEN"

Another luminary who turned my view of loss upside down was Maria.
Who would have thought a dying child would make me smile? She created
an upside-down rainbow in every way. Maria's light was her unbending
faith.

§

I walked into her room and there she was, tubes protruding from her arms
and her nose as she sat very still looking at the TV that was playing her
favorite cartoon. I could hear the steady *whoosh* of the breathing apparatus
as it sent oxygen to her small body. She and her family had traveled many
miles to get treatment for this beautiful little brown-eyed firecracker of
spirit for cancer of the mandible. After multiple attempts to shrink her
tumors, the physicians informed her parents that they could no longer
keep the growth at bay. Here she was with her cheeks puffed out like
a chipmunk, the tumors protruding on her face. I knew her time was
soon to come, and I came to say goodbye. A young social worker barely
understanding how to handle life, not to mention the death of a child
barely six years old, I approached her side. I stood there quietly searching
for some words to say when suddenly I heard this tiny voice squeak out,
"You came to say goodbye, right? I will see you in Heaven!"

As adults, it's easy to visualize a helpless child with tubes projecting
from her body and expect a withdrawn, dejected, forlorn little soul. We
might project our discomfort over her impending loss and likely imagine

her to have a sullen look and eyes withdrawn and cold. This was not Maria! Instead, I found a joyful and cheerful child who greeted me with smiles and a bright cheery enthusiasm about going to Heaven that took me off guard. How could she register any kind of afterlife or positivity at the tender age of six?

I came to understand that the younger we are, the fewer defenses we have developed. This little girl had not yet learned to question what she was taught. Instead, her Catholic upbringing taught her to trust that Heaven was going to be awesome and that we would all get there and join her someday. Expecting to sob, instead, I found myself with the widest Cheshire Cat-like grin. Her joyful essence was infectious!

To describe that moment is nearly impossible for me. Her spirit met mine, and together we shared an ecstatic connection that has lasted a lifetime. Maria died a few days later, and I cried as I grieved, but I also found myself celebrating her. Like Jason, Austin, and Walden, my luminaries were teaching me there was a ripple of joy that remained with all of us who knew them.

Witnessing Maria's love of life and laughter amid the pain and suffering brought a smile to my face even after her death. That was very confusing! How could a dying child bring joy? After meeting Maria, I was beginning to understand what Elisabeth Kübler-Ross meant about how the dying can teach us about living—even (or especially) dying children. Even a little six-year-old girl in the last days of her life on earth could light others up.

REFLECTION QUESTIONS

1. Does it surprise you that a child so close to death could be so positive?
2. What can you learn from her matter-of-fact comments about dying?
3. Can you see yourself accepting death the way Maria did?

CHAPTER 22

MICHAELA: THE UNSTOPPABLE MUSE

I affectionately call Michaela my "muse" because her tender heart was the image I most wanted to emulate in my work with dying children. But more than anything, Michaela became the embodiment of persistence. I met her on a day that will forever live in my memory: September 11, 2001.

§

Anticipating our meeting, I was driving down the major highway that led people from north to south across several counties in Maine when I noticed several cars pulled off to the side with people on their cell phones. I decided to explore what might be happening, so I pushed the radio "on" button and waited for significant news. Seconds later, I heard the shaking voice of the news commentator describing what sounded unimaginable: a plane that had taken off from Boston had hit the World Trade Center.

Without warning, like many on that September 11th, I too felt under attack. I was driving past the hotel where the terrorists had stayed the night before they flew to Boston, where their deadly flights originated. I was frightened. What if some of them were still there? When a plane flew overhead I found myself shuddering. Even now, as I write about that day, I can still feel my stomach turn into a knot as I reflect on what it was like to be so close to the scene of hate. I remember wondering how I could go on to my next stop, a hospital where I was to meet a child who had been diagnosed with mitochondrial disease, a neuromuscular degenerative condition that would eventually take her life. Balancing the tragedy of the world situation with the impending loss this family was about to face, I decided to continue.

As I made my way to the hospital where I was to meet Michaela, my thoughts wandered to the list of my relatives who frequented the Boston flight: my brother, my sister-in-law, and my nieces. I grabbed my cell phone, found my brother's phone number, and pressed the keys. My heart beating fast and my breathing speeding up, I waited until I heard his voice quietly reassuring me that everyone in our family was well. After ending the call, I pulled back onto the highway. After all, I had a dying child to visit.

As I walked into the hospital, I was not surprised to see groups gathered in front of the television, silently waiting to hear some message of reassurance. Instead, there was scene after scene of destruction and people leaping to their deaths. As stunned as each of them and fixated on these images, I decided to choose life, to go where I could make a difference. Amid the horror, I was determined to find and give light. I directed myself away from the lobby, following the blue line that led me down the corridor to the pediatric unit where I would find Michaela.

There she was, lying on her side in a hospital bed, her mother and father flanking her on either side. Her alabaster skin was marred by bruises from the intrusion of feeding tubes and needles— childhood battle scars from a disease that would eventually rob her of her life. To the naked eye, Michaela appeared to be suffering, tormented by the plight of a life-limiting illness, but her family knew otherwise. Offering a firm handshake to me, her parents took turns sharing stories to illustrate what they portrayed as an eight-year-old girl with a miraculous will.

To prove their point further, her mother placed a book in Michaela's hand. What I witnessed next dissolved any of my assumptions about her "dying." There was before me an unbreakable porcelain doll-like face smiling as she painstakingly turned the pages of her *Adventures with Froggy* book with her one dexterously adept finger on her left hand. I watched in silent awe as she listened to her mother read every word with an animated style befitting her work as an elementary school teacher. Testing her, Theresa purposely skipped a word, to which Michaela replied with a very loud, emphatic grunt. Despite her neurological challenges and reports from her neurologists claiming she had limited comprehension, it was obvious Michaela was far more aware than she was given credit for.

Her parents went on to share their building frustration as others focused on Michaela's weakness versus acknowledging her strength. One of the reasons they had called the Jason Program was the fact that our reputation amongst other parents was one of accepting and focusing on the way they lived, not how they were dying. We used to say we gave life to children's days. Her parents wanted her unique and valiant spirit to be recognized.

They were describing a miraculous child capable of extraordinary things. Primarily, they wanted me to understand Michaela "never gave up."

Her father recounted stories of Michaela participating in the Special Olympics. Accompanied by a support person and slumped over a walker, she made her way across the track until she tired. Exhausted but never defeated, Michaela used every bit of her strength to shuffle her feet as far as she could. I remember her mother describing a longing to lend her strength to Michaela during these times.

I was struck by the power of the commitment of parents like her mother and father, along with her siblings, who wanted to give everything they could to help their child heal. From the sidelines, they cheered and lent her their energy and their spirit of hope, and it was as if Michaela drank it up: it kept her going. Magically, in turn, Michaela's spirit inspired them and many others.

To the average person who met her, Michaela's body was not hers to master. It failed to allow her to be like her peers, to pull herself upright, or to put one step in front of the other, feats her peers took for granted. Undeterred by the setback she experienced with the Special Olympics, Michaela found a way to persevere: She abandoned the desire to walk and replaced it with a determination to crawl.

Theresa described a typical school day when Michaela would sit in her classroom with ten other students, content simply to be there in her wheelchair with her head slumped over to one side, her blueberry-colored eyes bright, her arms passively placed alongside the wheels of the chair, and her legs confined and still against the foot support.

One day, her mother surmised, there must have been an inner voice that spoke to her. Undeterred by her limitations as she sat on the floor with her peers, she reached out her hands and began to drag herself forward.

Crawling at first required strength she lacked, but after repeated failed attempts to make it across the room, she was finally able to push her way out of the classroom door. Imagine a hallway lined with bustling children bumping and tripping over each other as they hurriedly made their way to their classes. Chitchatting about their birthday party or what movie they wanted to see, they were oblivious to anything but being the first to grab a seat next to their best friend in the cafeteria. Then they look down and see her—Michaela, The Divine Miss M., aptly nicknamed for her superhuman capability. Right in front of their lanky legs and dirty sneakers, an unrelenting arm stretched taut, reaching forward to advance her limp, trailing legs another few inches.

Each day, as the bell signaled the change of classes, her classmates and teachers began watching Michaela routinely attempt to crawl her way out of the classroom and down the hall to the library, determined to reunite with her beloved Froggy books. Gathered on either side, they gawked at first, but as she persevered further and further, it became more of a spectator moment, and they began to cheer. Eyes widening and jaws dropping, they marveled at Michaela crawling past them. Each day, with great anticipation of how far she would make it, they would shout her name, her smile growing wider with each chorus.

She became a beacon of light for all who watched her navigate down that hallway. Each subtle movement inspired students, teachers, parents, and anyone who witnessed her daily attempts to make it to the library. It was as if her message reminded them that they were capable of so much more. Their eyes wide, their jaws dropped as she inched past them. A glass door was all that was between Michaela and her beloved Froggy books. With each attempt, she made it a bit further, and the gallery of onlookers was transformed by her determination.

One day, surrounded by her classmates, she made it all the way to the library door.

Arriving at the entrance, she moved with cat-like accuracy to the shelf where her Froggy books were carefully placed so she could pull them easily to the floor. Michaela stuck her hand out, and with two working fingers, pulled the book to her. Pulling herself up to lean against the bookshelf, she used the same two fingers to move the pages, gazing at the words and illustrations of frogs and their daily adventures in a lily pond. Anyone who ever met The Divine Miss M was struck by this fierce attitude of literally and figuratively always reaching beyond what anyone expected so that she could experience what brought her joy. And her spirit was infectious!

The students and staff became a participating community, assisting Michaela by moving her favorite books closer to the entrance. The librarian tearfully placed her Froggy books near the door and the entire school cheered her on, yelling great encouragement as she used every ounce of strength to reach up and pull down those symbols of her resilience. Remarkably, there is no scientific evidence to define what gave her the capacity to persevere. What allowed her brain to comprehend the book's messages? And most importantly, why did she never give up her quest to read? Unlike most children who struggle to utter a phrase, she possessed a yearning so strong it defied words—and yet she communicated her desire in ways that went beyond what her classmates who could walk and talk could ever communicate.

During her short life, she impacted the lives of so many. For those of us who grew to love her, it was difficult to make sense of her leaving this earth. I asked myself why someone so inspiring had to leave so young. For those of us left behind, the answer could only lie in how she lived, what she taught us, and the life lessons we learned from watching her master what to most of us seemed impossible.

Michaela's heart beat until she was 10 years old. As her body weakened and her ability to crawl diminished, she stayed at home with a caring and compassionate team of professionals and volunteers. She was surrounded by love and support provided by our palliative care team, her hospice, home care agency, a team of volunteers, and the local Kiwanis program, who adopted her family for a year. Because caring for Michaela was so challenging, her community worked together to raise enough funding for her parents to remain home with her for a few months. They also provided meals and took her younger siblings out to the park or for ice cream, allowing their parents time to rest or focus on Michaela's care. Our program raised funds for an adaptive lift not covered by insurance to be installed in her home. This meant her parents could allow her to lift herself up instead of remaining supine all day.

Michaela left us with so many luminous lessons. Her magic was her loving presence that without words sent a message that she was listening and watching. Staring with a peaceful angelic gaze and with her subtle, gentle nudges, she sent love out to anyone who lay down beside her. But despite her quiet persona and still body, there must have been a cacophony of internal choruses singing *"Don't give up"* to her conscious brain. She was unstoppable, and her magic inspired so many to attempt what they otherwise would never have tried.

Not surprisingly, Michaela died two weeks after a reading session during which she was unable to move her finger. When she could no longer engage her passion in her favorite activity, she let go and allowed her body to give way to peaceful rest.

Her memory lives on in a book-sharing program at the same school where she crawled her way to the library. Now there is a Michaela library program to offer other students the same opportunity to enjoy books that Michaela experienced despite her limitations. Her life has meaning as it continues in the form of others benefiting from her passion. Her passion became her purpose, and the pain she endured serves as an example that we too can endure unimaginable struggles and still find a way to enjoy life.

REFLECTION QUESTIONS

1. How does Michaela's perseverance motivate you?
2. If you witnessed her crawling down that hallway, what would you be thinking?
3. What is one goal you want to achieve that feels impossible? How can you start to address it?

CHAPTER 23

GRACE: "STOP THE DEATH TALK!"

Grace was the antithesis of what her name is associated with most often. She was irreverent, caustic, feisty, and at times obnoxious, but wow, I loved that teenager! She called herself an "angel with attitude," and no words could better capture her spirit.

§

She was one of those people who were grace-filled, not graceful. She had a heart of gold, but if you ever told her that, she would vehemently deny it. I met her in a nursing home because her debilitating chronic and terminal condition left her able only to lie on her side and back. She required skilled nursing care. One would think a sixteen-year-old living amongst aging adults would be depressed and depressing, but not this young woman. She spent her days barking orders at the nurses and physicians who cared for her and making the most creative craft items imaginable.

Lying on her side, her paintbrush in one hand and a small stone in the other, she created masterpieces. Ordinary rocks from the beaches of Maine were transformed into beloved depictions of the Maine landscape, illustrating the life she never had and never would. Her hand steady, she combined color and texture in precise strokes, painting detailed scenes of lighthouses or beaches or any other inspiring visual display from her imagination.

It was early October when members of our Jason Program palliative care team paid a visit to Grace—and she was not happy! Our physician mentioned the "d" word, and she would not have it. She responded with two very ungraceful words: *get out!* We were used to our patients' anger, especially when it was related to their sense of lack of control. When our doc brought up the subject of death, it reminded her of something she already knew but had no desire to discuss: that her battle against her disease was about to end. I knew she needed to feel empowered, so when I went to visit her close to Halloween, we came up with an idea.

I sat down with her, and with a serious frown, she mentioned the Grim Reaper. She wanted me to know that our hospice team reminded her of the Grim Reaper, and we really ought to stop talking about death.

We decided that instead of taking a serious approach to prevent our team from ever mentioning the "d" word in her presence, we would find a creative way to deliver the message in Grace's style. We figured out a way for her to dress up in a costume with a black cloak carrying the signature sickle to make a humorous but strong statement. When our physician came in to check on her in mid-October, she sat with a huge Cheshire Cat grin, sending her pronouncement loud and clear to stop the death talk.

That was a turning point in our conversations. We stopped discussing her prognosis and changing symptoms, which she never hesitated to tell you was boring. Instead, we began great conversations about finishing the 50 rock paintings that she needed to complete before Christmas for the 50 people who had meant the most to her throughout her life. We both knew she was rushing to finish her handmade Christmas gifts in case she died before December. She completed her list on October 30th, which was our last visit. She died on Halloween. Whenever that day comes along, I remember with fondness an angel with an attitude who is probably still anything but angelic. This beautiful person changed my understanding of grace. Grace can be messy and unpredictable—and can show up in a dark cloak carrying a sickle.

REFLECTION QUESTIONS

1. What do you think about Grace's attitude about death?
2. Do you think of creative ways to deal with challenges and limitations?
3. What is one lesson you can learn from Grace's approach to living?

CHAPTER 24

MAGGIE: SING WITH YOUR EYES

The glorious hues of red and orange were strewn together as if a child had taken an orange and a red crayon and blended them. The fiery glow was awe-inspiring in its grandeur as it spread across the sky. I started singing the words to the song "Sunrise, Sunset," the familiar words about life being filled with happiness and tears, joy and sadness, life and death. My first performance in musical theater was in *Fiddler on the Roof,* and I remembered the poignant message of this featured song written by Jerry Bock and Sheldon Harrick. The power of these lyrics and how music can transcend reminded me of Maggie—who, despite being unable to speak, exuded her light through music.

§

Arriving to see another child who was living at a facility intended for an older population because of her long-term needs, I ignored the fact that I wasn't seeing child-friendly colors as I made my way down the hall. With their cream-colored base and seascape paintings, the walls instilled a sense of placid calm that was appropriate for most of the population that resided there, who had lived a long life and were quietly entering its final phase.

I was here to visit a smaller representation of the residents. This was a long-term care program for older adults who shared space with a differently abled group of children. One of the children who lived there was Maggie. I was on my way to speak with her and her parents about how the Jason Program could help the care facility better meet Maggie's growing medical needs as well as support her family—for at the tender age of 10, Maggie was also in the last phase of her life.

I greeted the nurses, who directed me towards her room. Here was another child facing a life-limiting neurological condition that would eventually end her life. Whenever I made those long walks down a hospital hallway or an asphalt driveway, before meeting the children and their parents I made sure to come into a prayerful state of reverence and presence. I wanted to give each child the opportunity to enter my heart and mind with his or her unique story. Every luminary I met conveyed a different message to me. I learned from them that listening and paying attention to my whole body, mind, spirit, and emotions was essential in remaining open to what they had to say, often without uttering a sound.

The contrast between the hallway and this mecca I entered was striking. Maggie's room was like entering the Magic Kingdom. Posters of Princess Jasmine and Mickey and Minnie and other Disney characters were splashed on walls, surrounding her with a fantasy world. She was sitting in her wheelchair, her head upright and her arms holding on to each side. She was alert, and immediately fixed her eyes on mine. She exuded a smiling energy that I felt from my head to my toes. The moment my eyes met hers, we began, in our own way, to sing.

Maggie's mother, a 30-something petite, casually dressed woman, quietly approached me and sheepishly described to me how difficult it was to place Maggie here in an adult special needs program. She described how valuable the staff had been in engaging Maggie in activities whenever possible. There were markers and crayons and large white sheets of paper sitting on a table near Maggie's bed so that a nurse or a family visitor could help her create art despite her limited dexterity. Perusing the full extent of the room, something else caught my eye: a large CD player and a collection of CDs placed carefully near Maggie's chair. Maggie obviously loved music. I took note of this and began asking questions about her favorite songs and singers and how I could operate the player. It didn't matter that she was confined to a wheelchair or a bed or that she couldn't speak. I would find a way to sing with her regardless.

We take for granted our capacity for expression using the five senses. Nature, however, truly teaches us how to be present—how to pause long enough to take in the feeling of the wind softly whisking past our face, or listen to the occasional frog greeting us with his loud gurgle; how to gaze at the sky and imagine the shapes of clouds as objects we can relate to, and tell stories about what they represent; how to let the scent of the honeysuckle or the rosa rugosa fill our nose with their fragrance.

If I hadn't been the Green Mountain girl who spent hours surrounded by her organic teachers along the trails of Camel's Hump or the banks of Lake Champlain, I would not have known how to communicate with this level of understanding, which surpasses what we are taught. Thanks to those lessons in nature, I knew what to do the moment I met Maggie. Music became our anthem of connection.

Selecting a favorite Disney tune, "Whistle While You Work," by Larry Morey, Maggie and I began to sing, me with my voice and Maggie with her eyes and her smile. Her eyes twinkled like the light reflecting on a lake at the end of a summer day; her eyes *danced*. In that sacred space, we were sharing a passion. Sound transformed silence into a rich exchange of love. Without even touching, we were intertwined, moving to the music, me following her eyes as my signals to where we would move next. Like a dance partner, we were aware of where each wanted to move. When we sang together, she expressed a joyful simplicity with her eyes, as if to say with heartfelt gratitude: "My heart and spirit are singing and dancing with you, here, fully connecting with you."

I visited Maggie weekly for several months. I looked forward with great anticipation to selecting a different CD that would send us soaring together to a place that lifted and lit us up. For several weeks she was lit up like a Christmas tree; but like many of my luminaries, over time she weakened, her light dimming like a candle reaching its end. All too soon, she left us.

Maggie taught every person who entered that rainbow haven situated in such an unlikely place that magic was real. She exuded magic. The nurses described her energy as drawing them towards her with an inexplicable life force. They couldn't wait to come in and feed or clothe or bathe her. Many said it was the highlight of their day. How can a ten-year-old child fill a room with contagious delight when she cannot speak—when she cannot even move?

Maggie was my inspiration for the word *luminary*. She generated a bright light. If you were present with her, she shone like the brightest star in the sky that rewards those who take the time to look up on a clear evening.

I like to think of her dancing somewhere. When I look to the Heavens, I imagine her and all my luminaries with gleeful expressions, circling around, moving freely, and expressing themselves in ways they could not on Earth. Inspired by my luminaries, I don't take for granted my ability to do what they could not. I don't hesitate to move to any kind of music, to sing out whenever I desire, and to ignore other people's discomfort. It's not unusual to see me bebopping in church or a grocery store check-out line or when I am walking through the park. Life is too short to not take advantage of these moments. I dance and sing and love. Maggie taught me that.

§

REFLECTION QUESTIONS

1. Have you ever experienced nonverbal communication?
2. Do you think music and art is a form of expression? If so, why and how? Has it been for You?
3. Do you ever take your five senses for granted? How can you embrace them more in your life?

§

The remaining stories are about luminaries and their incredible mothers. I also met devoted fathers who helped support these luminaries. I chose to talk about the mothers because of the bonded relationship I had with them as a woman who had suffered pregnancy loss. The mothers in these stories became vital teachers about motherhood for me. Ultimately, what I learned from them brought me to my own experience of mothering. They taught me that the depth of love one has for a child sometimes means loving them enough to let them go when they are ready to leave this earth. Embedded within each of these narratives is a love story deeper than most of us can imagine. Despite what appears to be a tragic end, the ongoing ripples of this love last forever. Our first story is about MJ and Alex, who teach us the power of laughter.

CHAPTER 25

MJ AND ALEX: LAUGH WHEN YOU HIT THE POTHOLES

When Alex was born—the second son of two strong athletes—the future seemed destined to be filled with baseball, football, water sports, and a whole lot of fun. His older brother, Kevin, born 16 months before Alex, would be not just a sibling but a sports buddy. There was great anticipation for what life would hold for this strong, capable, blessed family.

MJ, Alex's mother, described the weeks after Alex's birth as an unraveling of this positive vision of their future as a family. Alex cried frequently, and his eyes were not tracking correctly. Intuitively connected to her infant, MJ had a strong sense something was not right. Her persistence in asking the right questions and allowing the medical team to carry out a battery of tests revealed that Alex had hydrocephalus, often known as water on the brain. The impact of this condition is brain swelling that can be painful and cause a little one like Alex great distress. The treatment selected was a shunt that would drain the fluid from his brain. Initially, MJ believed this would take care of the problem. Like any new parent, she wanted to look forward to the years ahead being filled with activities and milestones like the first day of school, prom, and high school graduation. She wanted to believe the shunt would allow Alex to experience a bright and active future.

Attempting to move forward as a single mother of two infants after the shunt surgery, MJ nursed and held and nurtured Alex and Kevin as often as she could. Even though Alex had different abilities, she found herself engaging with him on a deep level through touch and a sensitive, focused, attentive look that strengthened their mother-son bond.

Kevin, developing his own communication with Alex, grew attached to him and became a protective big brother. At three months old, Alex was diagnosed with failure to thrive and given a feeding tube. Kevin pulled it out in an effort to protect Alex from what was obviously not supposed to be in the nose of a child. An act of sibling love and protection, it was one of the first of many times Kevin would actively care for his little brother.

With the help of early intervention therapies and eye surgery, Alex was developing and emerging as a happy little boy. After a year of feeding tubes and glasses and multiple therapies, MJ had a pivotal experience through which she realized that she and her two boys were a family, and Alex's special needs would always be a part of that. She made up her mind that together, the threesome would enjoy each day to its fullest.

As an avid swimmer, MJ drew upon the strength and discipline she had garnered from sports and started engaging the boys in as many activities as possible. Alex, requiring special equipment they called his "stander," would watch as MJ and Kevin danced around him, occasionally reaching out to twirl his hands but always maintaining the eye contact that allowed him to feel included. Together the three went sledding and played baseball with Alex pushing on the bases.

There was a deepening connection between the three, and MJ realized Alex was communicating with her profoundly through his facial expressions, especially his eyes. One afternoon, exasperated with Kevin for his disruptive behavior, MJ disciplined him with a stern vocal reprimand. Alex, fully aware of what his mom's raised tone of voice meant, smirked, and smiled at his brother. MJ, amazed at Alex's level of comprehension, recognized at that point that Alex was developing a different kind of intelligence. Compensating for his challenges, he was honing his communication skills and learning to express himself. MJ described several looks that Alex used: his impish smirk, his happy and infectious smile, his pout, and his tearful "I-am-in-pain" look. Each became an expression of Alex's ability to emotionally connect and engage with others.

A woman of strong faith, MJ began to view Alex's special abilities as God's gift to Alex. People were mesmerized by what MJ felt was a

God-given sense of joy. MJ's faith told her that whatever talents and gifts God has given need to be shared so that they can make a difference for someone else. MJ began to realize that this lesson pertained to her. Once a fit athlete, she had become heavier and weaker and was no longer using her gifts and talents as a swimmer. She decided to embrace the family's combined gifts from God and began a workout routine that included both boys.

MJ began running, swimming, and biking with the two boys. Whether they were strapped into the bike seats or being pulled in the pool, the two boys gleefully joined their mother in daily activities that went way beyond exercise. Their time together was full of shared expressions of their special bond. One sunny day as they clamored along a bumpy road, they hit a pothole. Alex, momentarily jolted up in the air a bit, laughed, his face a wide expression of joy. Then MJ knew on a different level that her job was to face the speed bumps, hit them, and laugh. Unlike most, who often allow life's challenges to derail them, MJ's resolve was to laugh more, love deeper, and embrace every aspect of her sons' and her own gifts and talents and share them with others.

Committed to her new resolve to develop her athletic gifts once again, MJ began training and participating in triathlons with Alex. At the time, he was attending a school called Meeting Street, where he was able to interface with other children and continue his special therapies. The school was a vital aspect of Alex's social interaction with others, and that was important to MJ. She didn't want him to need her exclusively. It takes a village, and school was an important part of Alex's village.

When MJ realized that swimming, water, and access to a pool were important sources of comfort for Alex, she decided to bring together her triathlete competitions and the school's needs, and she raised money with Alex at her side to buy the school a pool.

One needs only to gaze at the photos of Alex and MJ competing in the triathlons, with infectious smiles and pure joy emanating from their faces, to understand their message. MJ describes how reaching outside of her pain to help others was the key to her and Alex's life becoming purposeful. She felt a sense of fulfillment and peace for the first time. When people who didn't know her found out Alex had cerebral palsy, their immediate response was to say, "I'm so sorry." MJ would be quick to respond, "Don't be; we are really happy." She believes that what happens to us in life is not as pertinent as what we do with what happens. How we choose to give from our differing abilities is a vital lesson that MJ learned from Alex.

At four and a half, Alex had a sudden complication in his intestines and died. Alex had touched so many lives in just a few years, the line for people attending his wake and funeral wrapped several times around the building. Even two mothers and their young children who had briefly met Alex and his mom on a ferry ride a few days before came to pay their respects. Alex's inspirational smile and joyful attitude had inspired and reminded the children of how grateful they were even to be able to eat food. The young mothers expressed their gratitude for the brief encounter they had with Alex.

MJ passionately believes that the joy Alex radiated came from a divine gift and that the "pure essence" of Alex is what continues to inspire and motivate her to help other special needs children. She continues to use her athletic gifts and talents to raise funds for Alex's school and has started the Alex Smile Fund. Through her efforts, his smile continues to make a difference.

REFLECTION QUESTIONS

1. How would you describe MJ's approach to parenting?
2. If you have a child in your life, how would they describe you and how you face difficulties?
3. MJ engaged Alex in her passion. What passion would you like to share with someone you love?

CHAPTER 26

AMANDA AND HALEY: A CHILD'S SIMPLE GIFTS

I first met Amanda as a determined teenager and several years later came to know her as the mother of a dying child. Despite all their pain and suffering, Amanda and Hayley offered unforgettable lessons in gratitude.

§

Amanda grew up in a spiritual community that dictated not only what she ate and whom she spoke with but also denied the truth when abuse became the choice a member used against her as a learning tool. She chose to take a literal leap of faith by running away from home and escaping a spiritual belief system that organized a world that was destroying her spirit.

She landed in my first private practice office, a tiny space with four bare white walls and two office chairs, barely enough room to fit the two of us. We focused on conversations about her life, how she envisioned the changes she would make, and what was possible. At seventeen years old, she possessed wisdom that left my jaw hanging during every session. She described in detail her beliefs about women and empowerment and her constant frustration when her ideas about equality and determination were dismissed by the members of the community. As she related their demeaning anti-feminist responses to her ideas, I could see her throat constrict. The thoughts being fed to her were choking her so much that one night she escaped, literally leaping into the darkness to find a way to be herself.

Amanda had never been given a birthday party. I began our work together with a celebration of her—a cake decorated with traditional birthday images that lit this young woman's face up with delight. Amanda went on to discover a life filled with her heart's desires.

Another manifestation of Amanda's gracious and fierce spirit was her daughter, Hayley. No matter how challenging a day had been or how downtrodden you felt, when Hayley entered your space, she lit up the room. Barely three years old, this wee cherub reflected her mother's indomitable energy to give and care.

Amanda called me several years after our work together had ended to get my support with another loss she was about to face. Hayley had cancer—a form of cancer that would likely take her life.

I remember hanging up the phone, getting in my car, and driving like a mad woman to the hospital. There, sleeping soundly in a hospital crib, was Hayley. I reached out and hugged Amanda as she sobbed uncontrollably, shaking as she voiced that guttural cry I had heard from other mothers and fathers of dying children. Dying with their child is the closest way to describe those moments for these parents. They hurt so badly, it was as if they were dying, too.

The Jason Program wasn't even a team at this point, just an idea of mine, so I took on the role of social worker to support Amanda and Hayley through those days. When she was awake, that twinkle in Hayley's eyes still brought a smile to your face, and her sweet disposition reminded me of what it's like when you savor that first taste of Thanksgiving: she always evoked pleasure and gratitude. Knowing her mother's triumphant story and seeing the seemingly effortless joy in this child's innocent face left me feeling profound gratitude. In Hayley's presence, you couldn't help but feel thankful for life. There was a brightness, a cheeriness even during the dark reminder of what was to come, that was infectious.

Amanda had bracelets made for all of us in the Hayley fan club. We wore them and held her close in our thoughts and prayers until the day came we had all dreaded. But Hayley, in her own way, made her last day on earth a gift to all of us.

I walked into the room where she was peacefully sleeping, her crib surrounded by family and caregivers. You could only hear silent, reverent breathing as everyone peacefully gathered to say goodbye. Suddenly, the peace was unsettled by Hayley lifting herself up. We were witnessing the unimaginable: a three-year-old was about to take charge of her own death.

First, she took her binkie, and walking around the crib, she gestured to all of us to place it in our mouths. Stunned and also aware of germs, we each pretended to do so. Then she grabbed a flower next to her crib and proceeded to stick it under the noses of all of us, and we of course followed her lead. Her final act was to grab her precious baby doll and hand it to the physicians who had cared for her. They cradled her as if to acknowledge to Hayley what a privilege it was to care for her. After one last hug from her parents and a final look around the room, she sat back down and made herself comfortable with her head on her pillow. She slept for a few more hours before dying.

After Haley's death, Amanda went on to live a life filled with her heart's desires. She discovered her passion for service, her love of nature, and her deep desire to make a difference in the world. Amanda became a nurse, and when COVID hit, the resilient spiritual muscles that pushed her to freedom guided her through harrowing days of self-sacrifice and service. She mothered a son and is a devoted member of her community. She transformed her grief into a resolve to live her life as Haley did: directed by love and gratitude.

Orchestrating her own appreciation ritual before she died, Hayley was a luminary who taught gratitude. Like her mother, she was the epitome of what in life is simple and utterly profound.

Whenever I think of them, I am reminded of the song "Simple Gifts" by Joseph Brackett: "Tis a gift to be simple, tis a gift to be free..." Amanda lived her life with gratitude for what most of us take for granted: the ability to be authentically who we are. The gifts Hayley shared in her last hours of life were expressions of what meant the most to her.

For me, the words to "Simple Gifts" are about what we learn as a child and struggle to rediscover as an adult—our inner dreamer. Simple living is living the way we did as a child, with a heart filled with joy and anticipation. Children simply live, and remind us, if we pay attention, that we can too.

REFLECTION QUESTIONS

1. What do you think about Haley's goodbye ritual?
2. Do you appreciate and express your gratitude to the people who love you?
3. What can you learn from Haley's mother about gratitude?

CHAPTER 27

TERRY AND HER CHILDREN: THE VOICE OF THE FAMILY

The children who have taught me the most about living were not just those who were dying or faced physical challenges. Some faced emotional obstacles brought about by adults in their lives who didn't understand their needs. One of the most frustrating aspects of being a children's therapist after working with dying children was developing unconditional patience with adults who had healthy children but struggled as parents. The following story is about one situation where the children and their wisdom forged a change in their situation. Barely old enough to understand emotions and relationships, these precocious middle schoolers were great teachers for the adults who would listen.

Terry had wonderful children, but complications in her life meant that she had to struggle to keep her family intact. She and her family maintained constant hope. She lived with the reality that any day, her children could be taken away from her, not because she had done anything wrong; she was a wonderful mother. She was, however, a woman facing the challenge of not having the resources to gain full custody of her children. Fighting hard against all odds, Terry and her daughters became a team, and together, they created a winning argument for why and how they should stay together. After a long series of legal battles, this formidable mom secured her family as a unit. At the heart of this victory was the children's decision to speak up and be the voice of the family.

When those children became young adults, we celebrated years of healing and new life. We remembered and rejoiced in the changes and growth they had experienced because they had persevered and with honest, desperate voices as children had proclaimed their needs to the adults in their lives.

Sometimes children beg adults to listen to them because they know in their heart of hearts what is best for them. In this case, a community of adults listened. Support came from their school, their neighbors, extended family, and the courts. They never stopped asking to be heard, and in their case, it made all the difference. They never, never, never gave up.

It's exactly what Jason meant. He believed that no matter the circumstance, even while dying, there is a path to love and belonging. As children, these young adults were given a second chance because adults relinquished their sense of knowing more and instead remained open to their heartfelt pleas. They have taken charge of their lives and learned the valuable lesson that speaking their truth is vital to their well-being. If one person won't listen, keep asking; somewhere, someone will hear you! Finding their village of support made all the difference for them. I have no doubt they will spread the light of love that they received from their supportive circle to others in turn.

In many ways, they epitomize what this book is all about: honest reflection, reaching out for kindness, and mirroring love. That's what builds the spiritual muscles to face our losses and experience our pain as a guide toward becoming our highest and best selves: who we are meant to be and who we need to be to give of ourselves to others.

It's that ripple from our losses that can make the greatest difference for all of us. Because as children they leaned into their loss and spoke up, they were surrounded by caring, compassionate people who saw their potential and valued them. If they hadn't gone through that turmoil, would they have become who they are now? I don't believe in a divine puppet-master God who puts us in these situations, but I have repeatedly seen the magic that occurs when love shows up within them.

We all have these losses. What if we could do as this family did? What if we spoke truth to power? What if we spoke our truth in love to whoever would listen and claimed our birthright to be loved and loveable? We can't stop loss, but what if we recognize it as a step towards discovering our potential?

REFLECTION QUESTIONS

1. Did you learn anything from the perseverance of the children and their mothers in these last three stories?
2. How often do you empower and support a child's voice and listen to their ideas?
3. When you were a child, did someone in your life lift you up by acknowledging and validating your needs?

CHAPTER 28

ELAINA AND MADISON: "HELP HER LIVE"

Sometimes, I am faced in my work with a loss so unimaginable it shakes me to my core. Over the last few years, I have worked with people who have been impacted by a specific kind of loss: suicide. I remember struggling hard to help Elaina overcome her desperation from the suicide of her daughter, Madison. I wasn't sure what to do. Then someone came to the rescue: Madison herself. The story of Elaina and Madison is a story of survival in grief and the discovery of hope.

§

When Elaina came to me after her daughter Madison died from suicide, I was overwhelmed with my own sense of helplessness. In psychology, we call it a "parallel process." I would listen to her tell her story over and over, feeling her palpable sense of sheer despair at what she could have done, her heart-wrenching self-accusations of "if only I had…" After she left my office at the end of each session, I would sit for at least half an hour in my chair, unable to move, wondering if I was offering even a sliver of comfort to this broken soul.

I learned many years into being a child therapist that sometimes, if I am still and quiet and allow myself to be open, I might receive a message about what is needed. I can't begin to tell anyone where these voices come from or why I listen, but as I try to comfort the families of children who died and I seek out a message from the dead child, a message comes. Madison was no exception. One day, sitting in my chair after a session, paralyzed from Elaina's recounting of her daughter's death, I heard that still, small voice: *Ask her daughter.* I silently turned my thoughts to her daughter and vocalized my request: "What do I need to offer Elaina?" I spoke to myself and asked for guidance from her daughter.

I kept hearing that my role was to hold the love in the room and find bits of hope. That didn't mean anything other than hope for survival for Elaina. So many days, she felt like her life was over, and I kept hearing *"Help her live."* So, I did. By listening to her story repeatedly and offering myself as a witness, over time she found a way to get up in the morning and choose life.

Now Elaina allows herself to enjoy life. It took several years, but she is once again living with hope. A parent who loses a child lives with a different concept of hope. A cloud hangs over their lives, and hope becomes moments of joy, experiences that remind them that their lives are deserving of love and nurture and belonging. Survivor guilt is very real, and though it will always come and go in her life, Elaina knows now that it doesn't have to mean denying herself the human need for acceptance. Her faith helped her reclaim her spiritual footing, and she said that it gave her the strength to give back from her pain.

This focus is Elaina's purpose and power. Emanating from her deep sense of loss, she has found a way for her daughter's life to have meaning by telling her own story to other families facing suicide loss. She helps alleviate their sense of being alone and validates their experiences. When a parent has a teen expressing suicidal thoughts, Elaina is the first to assist them in finding a therapist. She makes herself available to them until they are surrounded by the support they need to begin healing.

Her pain has evolved into a higher purpose that offers her moments of hope. Her story supports others, and for Elaina, that makes her life and loss almost bearable.

REFLECTION QUESTIONS

1. What are your biases about loss from suicide?
2. How comfortable are you talking with someone about suicide?

3. What would you say to someone after they lost their child to suicide?

§

In memory of Madison,
please become educated about mental health and suicide!

CHAPTER 29

KATRINA: "I AM A SUICIDE SURVIVOR"

In this chapter, I cede my place as author to present the words of another luminary: a suicide survivor who teaches lessons of hope. In her case, she became a mother to herself.

§

My name is Katrina Rose Bailey, and I am a suicide survivor. I am here today to support the youth and my community.

Suicide does not discriminate, and neither does mental health.

As a survivor, I know from my own experience how dark the world can feel. A misunderstanding may be that because I am a survivor, I am no longer at risk. Unfortunately, that is not true.

Research shows that when someone dies by suicide, at least six people are intimately traumatized by the death. Research also shows that based on the accounts of those who have attempted suicide and lived to talk about it, myself included, people do not die by suicide because they want to end their life. They die because they want to end the pain. They are battling an emotional agony where living becomes objectionable. A depressive illness itself makes it virtually impossible to hold onto any expectation of pain going away. While some may argue that a person who dies by suicide has done so by their own choice, I argue that serious mental illness or other contributing factors limit their choice.

I can remember that feeling, and I still feel it often. The difference now? I have the tools from training and my family and close friends. Even

134

my roommates have their own tools to make sure I am continually safe. This very idea of making a recovery plan used to make me feel uneasy. Guilty. Why should everyone around me need to spend their time learning how to deal with my issues? It wasn't until I forgave myself that I learned that "It's okay to not be okay."

It's. OK. To. Not. Be. OK. It is not your fault, and people who love you will understand that. Every day I apply the tools I have learned in recovery and therapy to make sure that at the end of that day, I'm still here.

We need to come together and offer teens the opportunity to change our world for the better. To talk about our emotions. It's vulnerable, which can be scary. But with the right training, speaking up and reaching out gets easier. We have spent too long not talking about it. How can we continue to not discuss one of the leading causes of death?

How can we stay silent when there is hope?

We need to reflect on our roles and on our attitudes towards suicide, our judgments. Our unintentional actions and unconscious beliefs contribute to a culture that minimizes the suffering of others. When we confront our own biases, we can help create change. We have the power to change the narrative by cultivating a community of compassion and action. That's what helps me every day, and that's why I am still here.

§

Katrina's words and Elaina's tenacity and faith are where hope lies. When we face unimaginable loss and find a way to transform that pain into a powerful purpose, we can discover hope.

For me, hope is not in a cure or a resolution or in fixing something that happens.

People die. People die from suicide, we lose our jobs, we lose our children, we lose loved ones. Hope lies in re-creating a life by acknowledging the loss, identifying our pain, finding our purpose, and directing our energy to helping others. It takes much love and listening, but when our hearts have been ripped away by loss, we *can* turn our lives towards purpose and live again.

REFLECTION QUESTIONS

1. How do you feel reading Katrina's story?
2. Have you judged teens like Katrina because you didn't understand them?
3. What is most important to remember about offering support to a teen in this situation?

A FINAL WORD ABOUT THE LUMINARIES

The luminaries in these stories and the mothers who loved them teach us about compassion. They found a way not to merely face loss and change, but to rise up from their circumstances and live to their fullest capacity, making a difference in the lives of others.

I call them "luminaries" because they illuminated in themselves and others an awareness that within each of us is an ability to cope with the most unimaginable losses and experiences. Many who bore witness to their heartbreaking challenges gained an inner knowing that regardless of our circumstances, we possess what we need to learn and evolve from our deepest pain into more compassionate individuals. We can all exhibit the resilient qualities of courage and strength that lit up these luminaries. When we witness this level of suffering, it reminds us of what is most important to us—connecting with others, caring for others—and we become more kind and empathic versions of ourselves.

Why? Embedded in each of these stories is a child struggling in pain and offering a life lesson from their triumph over suffering. They lift us up and light us up, serving as beacons to what and who we value. Somehow, watching a child struggle and overcome a barrier rouses a sense of our own strength and ability to do the same.

Each of these mothers made a bold choice to mother themselves—to protect, honor, and let go of their child. Loving and mothering is a complex dynamic that all of us can learn from and model in our own lives regardless of our gender. These luminaries and their mothers taught me that.

THE POWER OF BELIEF

When I think of these children, I am so aware of how they were able to focus their energies on what was possible—on what they *could* do—without the defended cognitive barriers that challenge us as adults. Imagine you could have the spirit of Ted Lasso and just *believe* without any encumbering *yes, but* thoughts. Imagine you could just be in the moment, consistently doing what felt right, unfettered by the thoughts or expectations of others.

Michaela didn't have a thought telling her she couldn't crawl, Maggie didn't know enough not to sing with her eyes, and Grace didn't care about how beautiful her rocks were. Each person whose story is in this book was motivated from the inside out, not by social rules or expectations imposed on them by others. They lived each moment doing what they could to the best of their ability. As Jason said, it isn't courage, it's have-to!

The ancient Greek word for *believe* is *pisteuó*, derived from *belief,* or *pistis*. The word *pistis* stems from *peíthō*, to persuade or be persuaded. The Greek word *pisteuó* carries connotations of deep trust and confidence. It means to believe, to entrust, to have confidence in something. It requires more than thought; it's a drive based on an unfaltering idea about what we *can* do. It's why so many people are drawn to Ted Lasso's character: his innocent, unwavering belief in a positive outcome even when his team loses.

What if we all adopted that kind of faithful approach to any event in our lives? The luminaries did just that. No matter how difficult their circumstance, age, or challenges, it was the *belief* that emanated from within that inspired so many of us who bore witness.

CHAPTER 30

MOTHERING A SPIRIT

I have agonized over whether to include this next story. My final decision rests on why I have written this book. If one person discovers a new way of living a more fulfilling life, including greater self-love, I have done my job. I have encountered so many people who have carried guilt from losses that they have somehow attributed to something they *should* have done differently. I call these choices the "woulda coulda shoulda's." So many people have said to me, "I do guilt really well." My response is always the same: "Guilt is useless." All it does is cause us to feel shame and despair. It brings us down instead of lifting us up.

I help people understand that if they knew then what they know now, and the circumstances were different, they might have done things differently. I remind them, "You did the best you could with what you knew and the resources you had at the time."

Whether it was not getting someone to the hospital in time, not knowing your child was sick, or not seeing the warning signs of suicide, people carry many losses with shame. I admonish all of you to release that heavy burden and instead *learn from and give back* from your losses. Life is precious, and the luminaries and their stories are like the amber alerts in our lives, screaming, "Forgive yourself and others and live compassionately."

Here is my own story of loss and its rollercoaster of forgiveness.

§

I wake up and pull aside the tiered eyelet curtains to reveal the snow outside. My roommate and I are alone in my apartment. I can hear her muddling around in the kitchen, the whirr of the coffee being ground. My eyes are puffy with that caked-on mess that reminds me how miserable I feel. I remember: *Oh yes, it's today. That thing I am going to do. It's real.*

I recall hours spent listening to "How can you even think about this?" Or "You are too young; of course you need to do this." Or my absolute favorite: "You will never get through this." Sometimes well-intentioned support can kick you when you are down. Everyone meant well. They usually do, but this was my choice and mine alone, and no matter how many times I agonized over it, there was never a clear right or wrong. It was one of those "road less taken" moments.

I gaze at the clock, a reminder that I only have a few hours left to imagine the "if only's:" if only I were... If only I had... If only there was... The list is long, and with each one, the knot in my stomach grows tighter. The excruciating difficulty of this choice is revealed in my blotched complexion and red eyes. There is no right answer.

Wouldn't it be wonderful if we could stop time and rewind to the point at which we could make a different choice? For me, it was an afternoon of playful sexuality gone very, very wrong. *It happened so quickly. I wasn't ready.* The excuses run rampant in my mind.

Remembering the *how* brought little comfort. The agony of the decision will haunt me for the rest of my life because regardless of the how and the why, the results will be the same. I sit on an oversized tweed-colored couch amidst the mauve pillows and ponder the impossible. Isn't there a way I can make peace with what I am about to do?

I remembered a lesson I learned many years earlier in Sunday School. *Where is the light? Where is the love?* The words were shared by a 40-something, married-with-three-kids, prematurely gray schoolmarmish teacher. I can see her gray wool cardigan sweater and corduroy jeans as she stands in front of us letting us know how important she felt this lesson was. The power of this image and her voice becomes louder and stronger as my thoughts cling to this idea: *What is the most loving choice?*

My beliefs about life and death and life after death and the spirit world all converge, and I see in my mind's eye an image of a cherub-like figure floating above me with a smile, as if to say, *"I will come to you when the time is right, but that's not now."*

I hear my own heartbeat, and time seems to stop. It's just me and this precious heart beating inside me, confirming that my life circumstances, the way the child was conceived, and the potential harm that would come in many ways meant that I am about to mother a spirit.

My choice is to love enough to let go and trust that the love I feel will get me through the next few hours. In that moment, we become a team for life, and we birth a relationship that survives to this day. I still speak with, connect with, and honor that ethereal being.

That bond allows me to rise from the couch, gaze at the circular maple clock sitting on the antique pine bookcase, and make my plan. The appointment is at 3:00 pm. Six-inch snowbanks flank the curb where the snowplow has pushed the excess to clear the roads. The snow still falling means navigating my way to the clinic will take careful timing, so I hurriedly don my down coat and trusty L.L. Bean boots, wrap my exposed skin with a scarf, and with a heavy sigh, walk through the heavy oak door.

My foot slips on the ice hidden below the accumulating snow, and I clutch the banister to steady myself. This will not be easy. Redirecting my focus to love, I make my way to the bus stop.

There aren't many people about; most are huddled inside, waiting out the storm, and as I pass mostly empty streets, this is somehow comforting. Making a lonely decision, one that you have heard others say to you is wrong, makes for a sense of isolation and loneliness that only someone making the same choice can ultimately understand.

I imagine a tiny heart inside of me that I am about to set free. This image propels me forward with each step from the bus to the clinic, each step a laborious reminder of the agony that has plagued me these last weeks: the realization that what I thought was my life's path has taken a vicious twist. Betrayed and overwhelmed, here I am, barely breathing and somehow continuing forward.

I arrive. No protestors! There's no one here to call me a murderer or judge me as if they somehow know me, to dig down into my soul with their lies about my choice being a deliberate selfish decision when it is anything but. Only someone like me can understand the agony that is this soul-crushing experience. I am so grateful those voices that haunt me with shaming comments are not physically here.

My chest and arms loosen, and I'm able to step unobstructed and freely into the empty waiting room. A stocky, middle-aged woman with salt-and-pepper hair and a reassuring smile reaches out to take my hand and lead me into a small room where I will meet with another nurturing woman, a counselor. She is younger, her petite frame, wire-rimmed glasses, tight jeans, and oversized sweater distracting me for a moment until she begins asking me the same dreaded questions that every medical professional asks, and I ask myself over and over. "Do you understand what you are about to do is an abortion? Have you changed your mind? Is this your choice?"

My face drawn and my shoulders slumped, I affirm my choice and conclude my statement about my reasoning with something that startles her. She removes her glasses, sits back in her chair, and reflects quietly, "No one has ever said that before. To describe abortion as loving a spirit enough to wait for it to come when the time is right." She is stunned by that understanding and conceptualization, especially from someone so young. She honors my words by gazing into my eyes and sending me a fixed look of validation. I feel seen, heard, and understood. That gives me great comfort.

Alone and overwhelmed, feeling young and vulnerable and insecure and helpless, the ounce of strength that comes from the wisest part of my soul speaks to me over and over. I do not want to bring a child into this world without the best opportunity for a wonderful life. I would rather it remain a spirit. I am certain that this is not the time for me to mother flesh and blood. I need to heal from the situation that created the fetus—not yet a child in my confused and terrified thoughts.

I sign the papers and wait. They bring me into a room where a very kind woman tries to speak reassuringly to drown out the sound of the machine. My flesh is tugged and pulled, a reminder of the part of me fighting to hold on. Longing to let go, I feel the sadness of loss. Afterward, left with heavy bleeding and a set of Kotex pads, it is over.

Gripping my throbbing abdomen, praying that I can get back to my safe haven, and fighting back tears for what I didn't want, I walk gingerly and determinedly through the snow, now even deeper. After what feels like hours, I grip the snow-covered banister, climb the steep stone steps, and collapse on the hard wooden floor inside my room. I feel like someone put a hot anvil inside me. I think that I desperately want to go to sleep and never wake up.

I consider that for a bit. Who would miss me? Why was I alone? Why have I allowed myself to be in this situation and have to make this excruciatingly difficult decision? A close friend even told me, "You aren't strong enough to do this." No one believes in my choice. I have no support, only judgment. *You were irresponsible, how could you, in these times there's no excuse...* Not one person in my life has uttered what I need to hear. My parents, my family, my best friend—I've convinced myself everyone would judge me. I am one of those "baby murderers." The circumstances don't matter. It will forever be my fault. No one will ever understand.

I lay there contemplating how worthless I am for a few minutes until something in my thoughts shifts to a comment my mother made when I was younger. "Hang on... someone will need you." She used to say, "When you have the worst of days, find a way out of it because you never know when someone will need you."

The pain is increasing rather than decreasing, and I am frightened. It's as if a light shines in the darkness of my spirit in that moment, and I find myself crying out, "Help! Is anyone home?"

My roommate's friend down the hall hears me scream. She rushes in, takes one look at me, and immediately takes action. She lifts me off the floor and calls the clinic. They walk her through what is likely happening: much like labor, the tissue is causing cramping. It will feel like giving birth until the cramping stops. The clinic calls in a prescription for the pain, and my Good Samaritan stays with me until another person brings the medicine. This young woman, whom I barely know, cradles me in her arms while I cry. She mothers me. There is no judgment, no shaming; only loving compassion.

She convinces me to contact my parents, who come without hesitation, never uttering a word about what has happened but giving me space to quietly heal. They sit quietly with me. Remembering my mother's comment about someone needing me, I realize that today is my niece's first formal dance. I want her to remember this special day, so I decide to occupy myself by creating a meaningful memento. I find a nearly new teddy bear and some black velvet cloth. I begin copiously measuring and cutting and sewing, and for those few hours, with my parents silently bearing witness, I create something new and promising from the pain of my loss. I decide to glam her up with false eyelashes and a set of fake pearls. I need to keep feeling like I matter, and by doing this for my niece, I feel useful.

§

Where is the love? I believe that God was very present when I made this decision. And many years later, when I was holding the hands of mothers losing their children—some making the same gut-wrenching choice because their child would likely live only a short time—I felt a purpose and peace emerge.

How we perceive the reason for our choices has everything to do with how we live and learn from them. This guiding force echoes in my life every day. I love by letting go and giving back to someone else, a life lesson that continues to motivate me and lead me through whatever changes and losses come my way. This was a life-changing loss and a life-altering beginning.

REFLECTION QUESTIONS

1. Have you ever had to make a decision that you knew would cause you a great sense of loss? If you were conflicted about this choice, what words of comfort did you want to hear?
2. If you were uncomfortable with the discussions above of suicide and/or abortion, what do you believe is the reason for your discomfort?
3. How can you be more empathic, accepting, and understanding of other people's more controversial loss experiences?

CHAPTER 31

THE AGONY OF PAIN AND BLAMING YOURSELF

No blood, no flow, aching breasts, and this feeling of fullness familiar to me...I was not able to allow myself to say it. But I did think it: *Could it be? Is it? Am I?*

I made my way to the drug store stealthily; I was protective of this secret. This time, I didn't want to pay attention to what might not happen or disappoint anyone but myself. I drove past the elementary school, where I sat for a bit, watching the children play on the jungle gym and the swings, watching their smiles and infectious energy as they enjoyed their playtime. I could see myself in my mind's eye, pushing one of those children on a swing, and as I got nearer to the Rite Aid in the center of town, I held that image. Me, pushing a child on a swing, careful to ensure that the slightest movement would not cause him or her to fall and injure themselves.

Later, as I entered that familiar bathroom where I had done this so many disappointing times before, I reminded myself that whatever appeared on this plastic stick would not define me for the rest of my life. I had to reassure myself that whatever appeared, I could handle. So, I gathered up my courage and peed on that little white piece of plastic that would tell me my destiny.

And there it was: the little blue line said YES! There was no one home at the time, and my excitement had to be contained until later in the day when John would be home. Then I could share the news with him as I had imagined so many times before. There would be colored balloons and teddy bears and streamers, and I would make his favorite meal so that we would both relish and remember this very moment. It happened just that way, and that night we joined friends to celebrate. John, in his foggy preoccupation with the news, managed to flip himself off a balcony, thankfully not hurting himself—but all agreed that becoming a father was definitely affecting him!

But as we both reveled in our future as parents after months of trying, a disturbing and unwelcome thought started to burrow itself into my mind: *This time, please this time, please, please, please stay.* Then I made a choice. No, I won't allow myself to think about this. Walking around with a sensation of peaceful and calm awareness of a dream come true, I was careful to not trip, not bump into anything, and of course, not overexert or anything that might harm this little life, this beautiful soul inside of me that we took to calling "Precious."

And yet, as much as I wanted to lie comfortably in a cocoon for nine months to protect Precious, I was a working woman, a social worker caring for dying children and their families. As the Executive Director of the Jason Program and the leader of a small team of health care providers, I was responsible for maintaining a non-profit organization that required my attention.

One particular day a few weeks after my discovery, I joined my staff in flying to present a seminar to a group of bereaved parents. As we gathered at the tarmac to board the private jet supplied by our client, I shared my news. We boarded the jet, enjoying every moment of our opportunity to fly to these families in such style, and my gratitude and enthusiasm almost blocked my awareness that my body was sending me a message. Fully in the air and underway, my stomach began to churn with a familiar, dreaded feeling: something was wrong.

As we reached our destination, I chose to ignore these sensations and move instead into the room where 25 bereaved parents awaited us. As the cramping worsened, I made the conscious and dreaded choice to go to the "little girl's room," as we often innocently call it. What I saw was the worst imaginable: blood, the flowing blood that was all too familiar from my other pregnancy losses. What timing. I was about to lose a child while speaking to bereaved parents. Do I continue? Do I stop? Do I tell anyone, or do I hold this secret? How can I impose my own loss on these people, who have gone through the unimaginable loss of their fully living child?

I took a deep breath and chose to speak to a nurse whom I trusted completely. She called the hospital emergency room and told them I would be arriving by the end of the afternoon. I decided I would complete the presentation and offer up my experience to these parents. Gathering my spiritual muscles, I delivered one of the most inspiring presentations of my career. There are very few people who can understand and empathize with the experience of losing a child. This group of bereaved parents didn't know that at the time I was speaking to them I was miscarrying, but I was empathizing with them on a cellular level.

Afterward, exhausted and pale, I shared what was happening with my co-workers just before they flew home. I stayed behind with the nurse, who took me to the hospital. They told me I had a 50/50 chance of keeping this pregnancy. I knew differently. I knew it was not meant to be. We found a hotel room and drank, waiting for the next day and the long drive home.

BREAKING FREE

We didn't know it, but this would be my final pregnancy. After that miscarriage hidden from the bereaved parents, the physical pain I was experiencing monthly, matched by the emotional sense of loss that recurred each month, became unbearable. For years, I had been told that if I just kept trying hard enough, I could have a child. *Enough*. I could no longer bear the pain and could no longer bear the emotional torture.

In the 1990s, there was a rise in clinics promising that holistic living and self-healing could change any diagnosis. If only you changed the way you lived, anything was curable. These well-intentioned practitioners sometimes sent a message that if we had any issues related to our health, it was pretty much our fault. I jumped through every hoop, bought every supplement, ate every "clean diet," and reduced my stress with every meditation. I lived, breathed, and spent all my money on self-care programs prescribed by one of these centers promising that I could heal myself. As my pain increased, the promises kept coming, and my guilt grew.

One day, the pain in my vagina was so intense I could barely walk. As I drove to a clinic doubled over at times, the words of those who insisted that I was to blame for my failed pregnancies stung me like a hornet leaving its stinger deep in my heart. I felt responsible for the children who were unable to live inside me. The "what if's" and "woulda, coulda, shouldas" rang in my thoughts.

Then I remembered the moms. The moms who had blessed me with their strength and their resilience, loving their children while knowing the loss was inevitable. Thinking of their courage gave me the strength and courage I needed to make a choice for a different and better life. I knew what I was asking for that day. I knew the choice I was giving up forever. But I was ready for a hysterectomy and the end of repeated loss and disappointment.

I entered the clinic, and my exact words were: "I need someone to cut this fucking pain out of me!" I had finally reached the point where I was willing to deal with the feeling of having failed my feminine role and face the years ahead as an infertile woman. I no longer wanted to feel the agony of disappointment every month. I was done with feeling like I had a hot anvil between my legs, in such pain at times I could barely walk. I chose to relieve the physical pain and was ready to be like a pariah in a world filled with families. I just wanted *relief.* I finally took charge of my health, stopped listening to well-meaning but toxic positivity, and called a surgeon.

When I spoke to the surgeon and described my symptoms, he immediately diagnosed it as likely endometriosis that had probably been there for a while. Endometriosis is a very painful disorder in which the lining on the inside of your uterus (the endometrium) grows on the outside of your uterus. When I shared the perspective of the holistic caregivers and how I had been advised, he graciously took a breath and told me that if I had only been reminded that allopathic and what is now called complementary care can work together, I might have been sent to a specialist sooner and not have gotten to this moment.

Of course, now we understand the need for balance, which is why we use the term complementary care, but back then, it was often one or the other. By the time I got my surgery, there was 20 years' worth of endometriosis reaching all the way up my spine.

The surgical procedure had been described to me as easy. I would be back to work in two weeks, feeling no pain. It was not to be. I guess I am one of those people whose tissue just loves to connect, and unfortunately, I developed incredibly painful adhesions—scar tissue that connects tissues that are not supposed to be connected. Lying alone in my bedroom, I felt that familiar burning. I was on fire. I cried and cried. At one point, I ran out and sat in the snow for comfort. It took a lot of pain management and patience to get through the initial surgery—and then hormones, because overnight I was in menopause. They call it traumatic menopause because your emotions become unmanageable, and you feel completely out of control. Not a pleasant time for your husband, who is also grieving the loss of his dream of fatherhood while taking care of his unraveling wife.

WHY ME? WHY THIS? WHY NOW?

Whenever we face a life-altering loss, we often ask these three questions: *Why me? Why this? Why now?*

As a therapist, it's always disheartening for me when they are followed by the words "If only I ..." Too often, we cling, to regret for what was never accomplished, left unsaid, undone. We believe we should have known better; we should have been better prepared for the unexpected. People naturally want to place blame, find causes, and attribute our fate to some logical reason. Instead of focusing our energy on what we *can* understand and the actions we *can* take, we direct our energies to trying to answer questions that have no good answers. To break free from this downward spiral of pain and self-blame, we need to respond with a different question: *"How can I rise to the challenge of this change?"*

For me at this time in my life, loss had a name: infertility. My body was not a temple, as many had told me; it was letting me down, and I began to resent it. Where I once found strength climbing mountains and riding horses, I now felt weak and inadequate. I went through a period of resentment that played out in not walking down the baby aisle in the grocery store. I avoided baby showers, and I couldn't bear to hold a newborn baby. Like many who face disappointing losses, I went through a long period of *why me?*

Until I remembered the luminaries. The differently abled children of the Jason Program embodied the spirit of accepting alternative ways of living despite their challenges. No matter their limitations, they found unique ways to not just cope with their challenges, but to triumph over those limits, discovering some skill, gift, or talent that enabled them to choose an alternative way of life. They understood, despite their limited neurological capacity, how to live each day as they approached their last. Perhaps you, like me, will find that dying children teach us how to look for alternatives, find the resources, notice the teachers, and leverage loss into an opportunity for growth.

REFLECTION QUESTIONS

1. Have you ever experienced the *why me* questions?
2. Do you have the ability to shift your perspective after loss?
3. What is one way you will choose to adapt a better attitude when you face loss?

PART 4

MOTHERING A LUMINARY

In this final section, I tell the story of another extraordinary luminary, our daughter Cali. Adopted in China when she was just sixteen months old, Cali has brought hope, light, joy, and an otherworldly spiritual sensibility into our lives.

But the road to mothering a luminary was a long and painful one both physically and psychologically. In the earlier sketches of my life, I spoke of the loss of my child soon after moving back east. Unfortunately, that was only the beginning.

CHAPTER 32

THE RED THREAD

Most people do not realize that adopting is a long, arduous process, but it's worth every single moment of effort. Once John and I chose adoption, we decided to adopt from China in about five minutes.

A Chinese proverb states that there is an invisible red thread that ties us to whom we are meant to meet. The belief is that this thread, no matter how tangled it gets, can never be broken. In Chinese adoption, this refers to when a parent and a Chinese child are joined to fulfill their destiny. In retrospect, the universe had been sending me signs of this destiny years before we adopted our precious daughter, Cali.

THE SILVER BRACELET

It was my twenty-first birthday as well as my dad's, since we shared the same birthday: July 6. I reached out and gleefully grabbed the brightly colored package with the golden ribbon. My dad had always given me silver symbols on big occasions, such as a key when I got my driver's license and a diploma when I graduated. Now, I was excited to see what silver symbol I would receive on my 21st birthday.

As I pushed past the green tissue paper inside, I found a plain silver cuff, a sterling bracelet that fit perfectly on my wrist. "Look inside," I heard my dad excitedly say. "It's engraved with our birthday!" As I turned the bracelet on its side, there was the date engraved—but it was wrong. Instead of being engraved "7/6," the bracelet had "6/7." My dad's face dropped and his bright blue eyes lost their sparkle as he expressed his disappointment. "They got the date wrong!" My mom, in her usual quiet way, piped in with "Well, that's the English version, they often invert dates." We all agreed that I would wear it as a symbol of the sentiment of the occasion.

For more than 20 years, I wore that bracelet as a reminder of my solid bond with my parents. Two decades after receiving it, that bracelet became even more symbolic when I learned the birth date of the little Chinese girl whom we would be adopting: June 7. During all those painful years of trying to become a mother, I was wearing the birth date of my future daughter on my wrist.

NEARING THE FINISH LINE

During the two-and-a-half years of the adoption process, my work with the Jason Program continued. During that time, I impetuously decided to run a marathon as part of a marketing plan to support the Jason Program. I hadn't considered what it would mean in terms of time, effort, or the obvious question of whether it was realistic that my 47-year-old untrained body could even do it. All that mattered were the kids who could be helped by the $20,000 of sponsorship donations we would get. Under the guidance of a wonderful trainer, I first built muscles and then stamina until I was able to run ten-mile and fifteen-mile training runs.

The marathon was a family event. My older brother Ron and my niece Alix had agreed to run the race. Friends and family were strategically positioned along the route to encourage me. My father, battling cancer, had desperately wanted to come, but his physician said he wasn't strong enough. We all resolved to run for him anyway.

As I neared the last miles of the marathon, my legs ached badly, but somehow, spurred on by the thoughts of everyone who had inspired and encouraged me, I started to pick up speed and even sprinted toward the finish line. Then, just as I was about to cross the finish line, I saw John pointing and jumping up and down, calling out "Look!" There was a little Asian toddler, a girl with pigtails flying, running in front of me until her mother grabbed her away. We had filed the papers to adopt a little girl from China, and both of us believed this was a sign about who was to come—a reward for all the times we held deep love and heart. Our long persevering marathon to become parents was coming to an end. Seeing that little girl was a symbol of hope for us.

ELEPHANT MOMS

I once wrote an article with another mom who had adopted a little girl from China. In this article, we nicknamed ourselves "elephant moms." Elephants have a gestation period of up to twenty-two months, and both of us had waited two and a half years from the time we first submitted adoption papers until we finally met our girls.

In the article, we described the ups and downs of waiting impatiently, not knowing when your dream of mothering will be realized, and experiencing periods of anticipation followed by crushing disappointment. For John and me, the lowest point came when SARS affected China and we were given notice that we might have to wait another year. I remember the tears I cried, sinking to the floor, thinking how hard it would be to garner the strength to wait that long. Then I spoke to another adoptive mother. She described the entire process as being like a rollercoaster: you never knew how long the ride would last, but when it did finally stop, it would be well worth it. Those words rang true for me and gave me a new resolve. Waiting patiently was the least I could do for the gift who was coming: a little girl to love.

By now, I had learned to believe and trust in divine timing. So, when a friend showed me the photo of another little girl from China who was ready for adoption, I quickly said, "That's not our daughter. We will wait for her. She will be born in our hearts. We will know when she comes."

Truer words never came out of my mouth. Several months later, with SARS raging, I started having this need to nest. I found myself rushing to the store and grabbing baby items—bottles and rattles and colorful bibs—and decided it was time to decorate the nursery. I had no idea why I felt this way; we had been told it would be months. Interestingly, John had a similar instinct, and one night he decided to go online and check for any updated information... and there was this affirming message: "There has been an opening in travel restrictions, and you will be traveling to China in two weeks!"

I heard him scream, and I thought something was wrong, but no, it was right, and within the next twenty-four hours, we received a photo of the girl we had waited for. Some voice had told both of us that she was ready, that she was there waiting for us to come, and we were ready to do whatever it took to make that trip.

The next day, I must have checked my email every five minutes, anticipating my first look at my sweet one: love in the form of a little Chinese girl. My heart was racing when, just before a business lunch with a colleague, I saw the email. I pushed the button on my Blackberry, and there she was, with a smile that lit me up. I burst into tears. This was my girl. She shared my heart. I felt a connection with her so strong that I literally could not stop crying for three days over the joy of our coming together. Even now, tears are streaming down my cheeks as I write this, and I remember with so much gratitude how incredible it was to feel loss for so long and then finally feel love for a child who shared my heart.

Now that we had a daughter, she needed a name. One day, John came up with the idea to think of flowers. What flowers did we love that would reflect our image of our Chinese baby? After rejecting the usual, like Rose and Daisy, John mentioned a flower that is not as common and stands above other flowers. We don't think of this flower in bunches, but rather as one that gracefully emerges from any bouquet: the calla lily. We both took a deep breath and knew that was it: her name would be Calilily, and we would call her Cali. I looked up its definition in Chinese culture and found that her name meant "Most beautiful." That was it: we had a Calilily waiting for us in China, and we would soon be her family.

REFLECTION QUESTIONS

1. Have you ever had to let go of a dream and found an alternative way of realizing it?
2. Do you hold a belief that helps you shift your perspective into accepting change more easily?
3. What have you learned from my story that will help you to make an uplifting choice—an unexpected decision that results in your happiness?

CHAPTER 33

ADOPTION DAY

I gazed out at the towering ginkgo trees, their green leaves hovering over the small fish markets dwarfed by the high rises. I had never seen so many people squeezed into such narrow streets. Rush hour was a flurry of perfectly coiffed hair and motor scooters rushing by the serenity of immaculately groomed parks. The clanking of the machinery utilized by men standing thousands of feet up in the air on bamboo scaffolding was a study in contrast: modern meets ancient. I could hear horns beeping as a stream of motorcycles wove past each other in a scramble to get to work. In the background were the voices of our fellow adoptive parents—all of us stuffed into a bus that smelled like rancid fish and sneakers after a run—on our way to begin a new life.

Nanning, China, a city of one million, was a study in contrasts. One minute there was the myriad of small businesses, the next, newly built skyscrapers. And then there were the parks, meticulous reminders of the daily ritual of the people here. Throughout the parks were small groups of all ages scattered throughout, some doing tai chi and others modern dance. It was that time of year when the goldfish were bountifully swimming in the ponds and the lotus flowers were still blooming. The last of the tourists were busily taking photos of the remaining colorful array of native Chinese blossoms.

Practically crushed against the window, I took in every aspect of those images that were part of my daughter's daily life. I needed to know everything. We had been instructed by the adoption agency before we made this twenty-one-hour trip across the world to learn as much as we could about what she had seen and eaten, her lifestyle, everything familiar to her. There were books on my living room couch about adoption, China, raising a toddler, Asia, Chinese New Year… I had been studying for two and a half years to understand every aspect of my child's world.

My child… the words seemed so overwhelming as I reflected on the months and months of preparation to get to this very moment. To be less than a few miles away from the courthouse where she was waiting for us seemed surreal. John, inches away from me on those two tattered leather seats, reached for my hand. He too was wondering what it would be like. Who were we to be entering this place and taking a child away from her home to join us? What were we thinking?

Then I looked down at my special bracelet. *Meant to be, destiny, Kismet*: there are so many words one could choose to describe how I had worn Cali's birthday on my wrist for the last twenty years.

The wheels of the bus squealed as it pulled up to a stately-looking brick building with its Chinese flag hanging from a towering balcony. Reminding me of the city hall in Portland, Maine, where we had come from, it looked official. As we entered, the halls were long and regal, filled with flags and photos of Chinese leaders.

We were greeted by a gentleman who ushered us into a conference room just past the entrance, where stood two armed guards. There was a formidably long table with chairs situated just a few inches away from each other and paper pads directly in front of each seat. We were told to sit, listen very carefully, and take copious notes. We could not miss a step or we would not receive our daughter.

Our hands shaking, we grabbed the carefully placed pen and began to write:

"We will raise our daughter to embrace her Chinese heritage.

We will not disparage in any way the Chinese Government to our daughter.

We will raise her to be successful and kind and a positive contribution to the world.

We will never harm her, hurt her, or take her life for granted."

One by one we wrote and understood the gravity of what was being required of us. That task completed, we were ushered past the many portraits on the wall, each slow step on the white tile floor producing a loud squeak. We must have sounded like a herd of elephants as we made the long walk to our destiny.

We entered what to me was paradise: an expansive room with a small stage in front and a group of Asian women holding infants and toddlers. Many of the babies were crying. I looked down the line and saw the familiar jumpsuit, the peach one. I had picked it and the matching sandals for this occasion because as anyone who knows me understands, I love "matchy matchy." There she was, her pigtail straight in the air, her brown engaging eyes and spirited facial expression that was crying out: "Get me down from here!"

Tears welled up as we waited for our turn. A small-framed woman with tender eyes who was desperately trying to hold on to an energetic, fiery-eyed sixteen-month-old toddler approached us. I handed this bundle of energy a stuffed animal—a striped, orange, calico-like kitten-shaped stuffy to hold—and then I reached out to embrace her. She would have none of it. She wiggled her way down to the floor and ran away from us.

We chased her around the room until gleefully she stopped and allowed us to speak with her. Looking into her large, dark eyes, we began saying the words we had been taught were soothing: "Gui Gui." As we repeated the words softly, she began to slow and eventually allowed us to touch her gently on her arm. After a few minutes of playing with my husband's camera, we were told it was time to go. How do I do this? Obviously, this bundle of endless charged energy does not want to be held. So I tenderly took her hand, placed "kitty" in the other, and we walked together out to the waiting bus.

Silently, she walked up the steps past the bus driver and the translator, who made several gestures to her in her native language, indicating she was to walk with us to a seat near the back of the bus. Her short, stocky legs continued past each seat where another child was seated. She seemed to meet the eyes of each one as she slowly walked past. Her grip became stronger, and I could feel her relying on me to lead her to where we were to go.

As a bonding and educational experience, we were taken to a museum where artifacts of our daughter's heritage were kept. Guards and curators in dark green army-like uniforms carrying guns met us and reminded us that these were the property of the Government, and we were not to allow our girls to touch anything. We entered, each of us gripping our daughter's hands, and after touring the ancient knives and pottery and paintings of scenes of people in large fields gathering rice, we decided to attempt our first meal in the museum cafeteria.

The only thing we recognized was chocolate ice cream. I protested vehemently: "John, no, what if she smears it everywhere?" But John proceeded to grab a cone and hand it to our daughter. Her lips widened and her face opened, and she took hold of that chocolate that was forever to be the object of affection that first bonded us. Yes, she got it all over her outfit, and yes, it was sticky, and yes, we had to hold on to her tightly to keep her from breaking the rules, but to this day we tell the story of how that ice cream brought us together.

The first night included another meal. We gave her soy milk for the first time—different from the constituted milk powder she was used to— which proved to be not only yummy for her but also had a soothing effect. She took a sip, took several bites of her soup, and slowly her eyes began to droop. With each bite she moved slower, until eventually, she fell asleep right over her bowl.

We laughed and then wondered, "What do we do now?" It was time to carry her for the first time. Reaching down gingerly to pick up this sleeping angel, I lifted her and allowed her head to lean over my shoulder. I sat for a moment and relished the sensation, feeling on a cellular level what I had longed to experience for so many years. To love a child, to hold a child, to feed a child, to be responsible for a child—this moment was when I first realized that years of loss had led us to this moment, the realization of a dream. My eyes met my husband's, and our shared gaze spoke volumes. All the paperwork, the waiting, the interviews, the fingerprints, the essays—it all led us here, to family.

Even though we had given her the name Cali, we decided to alternate between her Chinese name and Cali so she would understand we were referring to her. I can only imagine how confusing all of this was. Everything changed for her in a matter of moments. Her food, her name, the people caring for her—how traumatizing it must have been. Being therapists, we understood when we chose to adopt internationally that this little one would have to adjust to major changes and losses. So, we promised ourselves we would be very patient in expecting her to bond with us. The ice cream helped but we had a long way to go. We were up for the challenge!

We made it to the hotel room, where we had our first experience of changing her diapers. Seated strategically on the edge of the bed, I gathered the ointment and diaper and reached for our now squirming child, who was busy playing with a newspaper she had found sitting on the night table. Unfortunately—or maybe not—as I reached for her and tried to put her down, I fell backward, doing a complete backward somersault off the bed. She and my husband could barely breathe, they were laughing so hard. Well, if it took Mom being acrobatic to produce this glee, then so be it! Lying for a few minutes watching as this little round face peered over the side of the bed, probably wanting me to repeat this maneuver, I stayed there and wondered at how I felt: the absolute sense of wanting the world to stop in this moment so this experience would never end. My heart was so full of love and joy.

The next day, we were once again seated in an airplane with twelve seats across. I could barely move, and much to the chagrin of the passengers in business class, this flight carried at least twenty infants. The gentleman in front of us looked back, saw the busy little hands behind him, and sighed. John and I waited until the flight attendant read the safety instructions in English, then grabbed the goldfish crackers, boxes of soy milk, puzzles, and games we had purchased in the airport gift shop for two-year-olds, and took a deep breath. We had done it. We were parents. As the plane took off into the sky, we held each other's hands and cried tears of exhaustion from years of anticipating this moment. We had no idea what lay ahead of us, but we knew in that moment we were blessed.

Once we stepped onto American soil, our adoption was final, and Cali was an American citizen. My brother and sister-in-law greeted us as we walked into the San Francisco airport. After a meaningful visit and some much-needed rest, it was time to say goodbye to our treasured family and bring Cali to Maine, her new home. We said our goodbyes at the airport and made our way with Cali, in her stroller with bright pink and orange flowers, to the gate where we were to board a flight to Philadelphia. There was a couple, probably in their early forties, who were staring at us. I couldn't help but notice because they were pointing at her and smiling.

We hadn't been back in the US long enough to understand that this would be a common occurrence throughout Cali's life. Many strangers stared at our family, and some were brazen enough to ask if we were going to teach her the violin or if she was good at math. This was not the case here, though. This couple was staring for a reason. As fate would have it, they showed up again on our flight to Philadelphia and sat right across from us. They had been considering Chinese adoption, and watching us felt to them like a sign that perhaps they were meant to do this.

We chatted about the process all the way from California to Pennsylvania. I shared the proverb of the red thread with them, and they agreed that our meeting was no coincidence. When we left them in Pennsylvania, we exchanged addresses, and several months later, we received a card saying that they were leaving for China to adopt their little girl. The red thread continued. There was just so much magic surrounding our little girl and her adoption.

REFLECTION QUESTIONS

1. What do you think of the bracelet and the red-thread concept?
2. When you feel helpless, how do you rediscover hope?
3. What does this story teach you about how you want to live?

CHAPTER 34

OUR LITTLE TEACHER

I have come to recognize that I am mothering a wise teacher. Cali's red thread led her to us for a reason. It was destined. And the entire process of learning from the losses of infertility and the choice to adopt has certainly been a re-creation of my life.

Cali has layers of loss that she must face, and yet there is some indomitable spirit within her that keeps her loving and learning and growing more aware of who she is and wants to be. In many ways, her life parallels her adoption: full of ups and downs and disappointments and pain, and then those moments when she, like us, arrives home to ourselves.

There has been much written about the trauma of adoption and the impact of relinquishing children from their biological parents. Cali is no exception. Her traumatic loss of anything familiar included being confined in a crib when she had been raised in the same room with her foster parents on a mattress placed on the floor near them. Suddenly, she was not only in a room by herself but inside something that held her behind bars. She couldn't see us or hear us or get to us. She couldn't wiggle or squirm or move around as she had on the floor. We learned very quickly, after she acrobatically pulled herself out and flipped herself over several times, that the crib was not going to work. She screamed inconsolably until we opened her door so that she could easily get up and run to us whenever she needed us.

There have been losses and layers for her to learn about and cope with, and she is still doing that hard work. Cali, unlike most of us who grew up before mental health and trauma treatment was recognized, is being taught to face every loss wholeheartedly and authentically.

Just as her story is one of loss, learning, and growth, so too is her adoption story the greatest miracle of my life.

When we first brought Cali home to Maine, we knew from the first moment that this little being was also going to be a teacher. She had cried and screeched from Philadelphia to Portland, Maine. We tried everything—food, rocking her, walking with her, singing to her—and she would have none of it. We finally just held her and let her cry, recognizing that she was probably scared and grieving that she had been taken away from anything familiar in her life.

When we walked through the door into our living room, John and I collapsed onto the couch, and our beloved friend Joyce, who had been there to greet us, swooped Cali up in her arms. Relief: maybe now she would stop crying? But no, not right away… until her head became very still, and she looked towards the stereo where soothing jazz music was playing. Cali jumped down from Auntie Joyce and walked towards the music. Then she began to sway as if she was entranced by the sound. Not only did she stop crying, but she danced and smiled and started cooing this toddler Chinese language we were slowly trying to understand. From the very beginning of our life with her, Cali was showing us that music soothes us, and that no matter how upset you are, you can dance your way through it. She and I used to say, "When in doubt, dance out."

THE MONKS OF HAWAII

We knew we had a spiritual child, and both of us were committed to offering her the space to be that luminous child.

The spirituality of our child was more than confirmed by an amazing experience in Hawaii. By the time we left for a vacation in Hawaii, we had been parents for over a year, so we had a bit more confidence—but a six-hour flight across the country, followed by another six hours out to Hawaii, was a bit daunting! The first leg to LA went fine, but as we took off for Hawaii, it started. We had absolutely no idea what triggered her sadness, anger, or both, but Cali started screeching. It lasted until she finally exhausted herself to sleep. The same kind of episode had happened several times before at home and happened again in Hawaii. Later, our clever pediatrician reminded us that planes are associated with leaving behind people she loves, and she was likely feeling abandoned. That's an internalized loss for Cali—a loss so deep that she would cry inconsolably at times for hours that first year after we brought her home from China.

We finally arrived on the island, and after a good day of rest and another fun day at the beach, we decided to visit a local monastery. A friend who had flown over from Honolulu thought we would enjoy the beauty of the gardens. It was exquisite—the lush green cascading plants and serene water with peaceful, bright floral displays left one feeling content to sit and take in the surrounding beauty. We three adults did just that. Seated on a bench, we began a commentary on the flora and fauna—until we realized Cali was no longer playing in front of us. Overcome with that instant can't-breathe, heart-racing parental terror everyone has felt when they can't find their child, we began to rush around, dodging others as we made our way around the grounds desperately looking for her little floral dress with the pink flowers.

Thankfully, she hadn't gone far. Around the corner from where we sat, a group of Buddhist monks had entered a sanctuary, and Cali, for whatever reason, had followed them there. She was seated in a full lotus position, her little toddler body now fully calm and peaceful in a state of prayer. To say we were stunned is quite an understatement! We three adults stood and watched quietly and reverently as she followed the lead of the monks who surrounded her. They paid no attention, but I am sure they were aware of her.

She caught our eye and gleefully ran back to us. Her nickname, "Calibabba," given to her by my best friend Marie, was born that day! Cali had shown all of us that the innocence of a child can allow an undefended spirituality that all of us could learn. She was still connected to something beyond her in that moment with those monks. How? Why? All we knew was her hyperactive little feet and hands that never stopped were calmed in the midst of those calm, meditative souls.

The little one I call my sweet one exuded the same kind of joy that I had known in all my luminaries. She even came to know some of them. One day, when I was about to leave for the hospital, six-year-old Cali met me at the door and told me, "Send them to their own cloud, Mommy." She understood in her own way that I was supporting them as they died.

As she has gotten older and faced her challenges and losses, it has become more and more clear that our most important role is to nurture Cali's spirit. Like all the mothers whose stories I have shared in this book, when your child is struggling, a parent rises and uses whatever tools they have, whatever wisdom they possess, and whatever resources they need to lift that child up.

The day I became a mother and looked into the big brown eyes of my precious Cali, I fully understood the courage of those mothers. I know that their hearts still ache for their children who have passed on, and I often think of Cali's birth mother. She doesn't even know where Cali is. There is a price to mothering a luminary, and yet not one of those women would have ever wished that they didn't have their child, even for the short time they were granted. Because mothering is forever.

At some point, there is a challenge that calls a mother to garner every ounce of strength in her spiritual muscles, dig deep inside of her, and choose to bring the best she can to loving her child and making every moment of their life count. Sometimes that involves the strength it takes to bring them into the world. For others, it means the strength to guide them as they leave it. The mother of a luminary must garner all her reserve power every day to focus on what lights up her child.

The mothers in the stories of my luminaries all did this. They made an enlightened choice to live according to what mattered most to them: their child's quality of life. In some cases, they knew their child's life would be shortened, and they were motivated to bring moments of hope and joy to their child, despite their child's limited ability to participate in what other kids were able to enjoy. No matter the obstacle, whether it was their child's inability to walk or talk or even their impending death, these mothers rose up and took charge and became the mothers their children needed.

My own story is also one of determination, even when living in the hell of loss. Like all these mothers, I found a way to cry out, get help, and keep going. That is the message from the amazing mothers of luminaries: None ignored the pain of their experience; they made it a catalyst to bring joy. They were able to look at their loss as a way of discovering and re-affirming what is to be honored and valued in life.

REFLECTION QUESTIONS

1. How can we adopt an uplifting attitude when our possibilities are limited?
2. When faced with an obstacle to your dreams, have you been able to embrace an alternative way?
3. What lessons can you learn from the mothers of the luminaries?

CONCLUSION

I am gazing at the white-capped Olympic mountains, the sun is shining on the water, and I am writing and reflecting on this wonderful ride of a life I have led. We live now on the other side of the country from New England. I am re-creating a new life with John and our daughter Cali. Looking out where the water meets the sea, John and I are re-creating ourselves in our private practice, Recreate Coaching and Counseling. It will come as no surprise to anyone who reads this book that the luminaries and their families have led me to this place. I have converted the passion I hold for these precious teachers into a way of supporting people as they transform their lives.

All the stories in this book, including my own, illustrate the cyclical process of returning to our sources of strength and wisdom when life circumstances seem unbearable. In times of loss, there may come a miraculous moment when hope shifts and we rediscover what we knew in the womb and as young children: the purpose of life is to love and to make a difference

The process of re-creation each of us relives repeatedly is the cyclical experience of transforming pain into a purposeful life. Each day, we have moments of all types of discomfort. If we learn from children, we take these miraculous moments as an opportunity to be present in tender, vulnerable love with ourselves and others.

"You knew, but then you grew up." Austin was definitely on to something. I hope that as you have explored these stories, you have discovered everyday life principles you can use as you encounter large and small losses throughout your days.

You have read examples of people just like yourself who have faced loss and made a conscious choice to experience all four aspects of their reactions: physical, emotional, mental, and spiritual. As a result, they allowed their discomfort to indicate what they value, and they formulated a strategy to re-create themselves in such a way as to fill their unmet needs in a new way. Their transition through loss has allowed them to become wiser, more compassionate versions of themselves.

They re-created themselves. My conceptualization of this process is called the Re-Create Cycle of Loss Change and Growth. It emanates from my transformation through the many deaths and losses I have incurred as well as those of others whom I have witnessed. Thanks to the many teachers who have graced my life with such wisdom and knowledge, transforming pain into a purpose-filled life is the focus of my work.

I have watched as the smallest of lives in the shortest of durations have inspired others to go through the phases of re-creation. With each phase, I have grown to understand the power of embracing loss as an opportunity to gain awareness of the skills, gifts, and talents we have to share.

One of my favorite lessons from Jason is that once he knew he had cancer, he realized he needed to make his life count. He did, Austin did, MJ did, Michaela did—and the list goes on. There is not a day that goes by that I am not thankful for all of my teachers. And now, as I gaze out at one of the most beautiful nature scenes imaginable, I am at peace because I know I have used the gifts I have been given to better others. Just as the water sits placidly before me, so does my heart. I have given what was given to me back to the world. My heartfelt hope is that in my own small way, I have honored these teachers and luminaries by telling their stories, and made a difference.

Thank you for reading UPLIFTING!

Please share your feedback on social media using any of the following hashtags: #uplifting, #DrKatie Eastman, #re-create, #loss, #change, #growth, #grief

If you enjoyed this book, please consider writing a review with your honest impressions on Amazon. Your feedback is incredibly valuable for helping an independent author like me to reach a wider audience.

To learn more about my services and my Re-Create tools please visit my website at www.drkatieeastman.com

You can also find me on social media at:

Instagram
https;//www.instagram.com/drkatieeas

Linkedin
https://www.linkedin.com/in/keastmanpsydlcsw/

Facebook
https;//www.facebook.com/DrKatieeastman

Or you can email me directly at drkatie@drkatieeastman.com
Be in touch!
I would love to hear from you!